AF344883

"THIS IS A MIRACLE"
SAID MY DOCTOR

REVERSING HAIR LOSS AND ALOPECIA

Selim Dursun

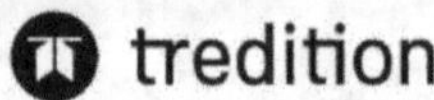

© 2023 Selim Dursun

Website: www.hawloo.eu

Verlagslabel: Hawloo, www.hawloo.eu

Druck und Distribution im Auftrag des Autors:

tredition GmbH, Heinz-Beusen-Stieg 5, 22926 Ahrensburg, Germany

ISBN
Paperback   978-3-384-06343-4
Hardcover   978-3-384-06344-1
Großschrift   978-3-384-06345-8

Das Werk, einschließlich seiner Teile, ist urheberrechtlich geschützt. Für die Inhalte ist der Autor verantwortlich. Jede Verwertung ist ohne seine Zustimmung unzulässig. Die Publikation und Verbreitung erfolgen im Auftrag des Autors, zu erreichen unter: Selim Dursun, Fichtestr. 65, 63303 Dreieich, Germany.

Alle Rechte vorbehalten.

Selim Dursun

He was born in 1990 and raised in a small town called Deggendorf in Germany. He graduated from high school with a major in psychology and education. He then spent six years in Istanbul where he successfully obtained a graduate degree in theology. After returning to Frankfurt, he completed his master's degree in religious studies at Goethe University. He pursued his studies out of pure passion and has no intention of ever earning a living pursuing them.

Professionally, he has worked as an integration teacher and is active in the field of online commerce and marketing. But his true passion belongs to art, especially film. With dedication and commitment, he has developed and specialized in this field. By attending special courses on short film production and photography, he was able to deepen his knowledge. He is the director of a short film as well as numerous commercials and is also active as an author and Youtuber. His goal is to always create useful works that contribute to the personal development of both himself and others.

This book is dedicated

... to my mother, whose unwavering spiritual support throughout my entire healing journey has been invaluable.

... to my father, who has generously provided unwavering financial assistance, I am forever grateful.

Thank you both

for your unconditional love and support.

Content

I would like to express my heartfelt gratitude

to my dear friends and brothers

Mehmet Karadeniz, Mehmed Çakır and Sami Aslan,

who graciously reviewed the English version of my book. Their meticulous attention to detail and valuable feedback greatly contributed to the quality and accuracy of the final product. I am truly fortunate to have friends like them who not only support me but also go above and beyond to help me succeed.

Thank you for your unwavering support and dedication.

I would also like to express my sincere gratitude to all the wonderful people who motivated me, supported me and contributed significantly to the creation of this book. A special thanks goes to my friend Bayar Bayrakcı, who was the first in this regard.

At this point I would like to thank my many good friends like Ziya Pasha, Savas, Murat, Burakhan, Iskender, Enes, (again) Mehmet, Ömer, Ahmet and many others from the bottom of my heart. During my illness, they not only supported me psychologically, but also were always there when I needed them. Their unwavering friendship and unconditional support sustained me during the most difficult times and helped me overcome my challenges.

A special thank you also goes out to my friends who may not have been mentioned by name, but have nonetheless made significant contributions to my recovery and well-being.

You have shown me that true friendship knows no boundaries.

May our friendship continue to grow and blossom, and may we share many happy and healthy times together.

From the bottom of my heart, thank you.

INTRODUCTION

Dear reader,

I never thought that my illness would eventually turn into a valuable and useful book.

If you suffer from hair problems or fear to face them in the future, this book is for you a comfort, a hope, a comprehensive guide and an absolute treasure of valuable and applicable knowledge. In this book, you will be surprised and thrilled to learn how to prevent and reverse hair loss. Moreover, you will realize that these methods are not only beneficial for the hair, but also for the overall physical health. You will understand that hair loss is only in very few cases due to genetic causes and that our body signals us through extraordinary hair loss that something is wrong.

This book is the result of my long, self-tested methods and therapies for hair growth. It is the result of my long research. I will tell you how and why I did not give up after four years of struggle for my health, although after years of therapies my doctor told straight to my face that there was nothing more he could do for me.

This book will give you the motivation to fight for your health and not to give up. This motivation will not only be emotional and therefore transient, but also rational and therefore persistent, which is why it will give you the strength to continue.

No matter in which subject, if you want to be successful in one profession, mindset makes 80% of it. Therefore, in this book I have not only presented the practical and technical side of it all, but also the theoretical side, in which my mindset played a very important role. My mindset has been formed from my beliefs. Even though not everyone shares the same beliefs as I do, everyone knows that it is a proven fact in the medical world that faith is a very important factor in fighting diseases (keyword: placebo). Some people say that they were healed by chance because of their faith, while others believe that they were healed by a divine power because of their faith. But in either case, it is obvious how important a faith is. So if I had not written about my faith in this book, much of my healing story would have been incomplete. But even if you and I don't have the same faith, I hope that my faith will give you some new and useful insights. Yes, this book is not only for people of my own faith, but for all members of the human family.

However, I hope that by sharing my perspective, it can provide you with fresh and insightful viewpoints, regardless of our differences. Therefore, this book is intended not only for individuals of my own faith, but for all members of the human family who may read it.

Amidst the pages of my book, I want to share a very special surprise with you. It is a foreword not written by me, but by a person who has a unique perspective on my story. My physician, Prof. Rudolf Schopf, MD, has generously written a valuable foreword for this book. It fills me with great honor to be able to share his words with you. In doing so, I have decided to place his foreword not at the beginning, but at a very special place in my book.

This book is divided into two chapters. The first chapter is titled "My Healing Story" while the last chapter is titled "Your Healing Story" and describes the natural treatment method that will hopefully lead to your healing.

Who is this book for?

- For everyone who suffers from hair loss, is looking for a sustainable solution to this problem, and is ready to fight.
- For those who fear to face hair problems in the future.
- For those who will be excited to discover a groundbreaking new cure in modern medicine for the disease Alopecia Areata.
- As an alternative to hair transplantation for those who are looking for a much cheaper solution that is natural and permanent.
- For those who still have problems with hair loss despite hair transplantation.
- For all those who want to think not only about the health of their hair, but also about the health of their entire body and mind.
- For all those who are struggling with an illness and long for renewed strength and vitality.
- For those who want to gain the secret knowledge of how to look and stay younger and healthy in today's world.
- For anyone who wants to share in an extremely interesting healing story and learn valuable lessons.
- For anyone looking for an exciting insight into the health care industry and to gain valuable new knowledge.

This book offers a diverse perspective that will appeal to people with specific hair problems as well as those interested in general health and wellness. It also appeals to those looking for inspiration, insight, and a deeper understanding of the health industry.

Additional material and support

New! All my recommendations through one link

In order to provide support to my readers, I will be providing links and QR codes to various recommended remedies and articles throughout this book. If you make a purchase through these affiliate links, I will receive a small commission from the seller, but you will pay the same price as usual. Of course, you are not obligated to buy my selected products and you can choose any other products you like. I have carefully selected the products and almost exclusively linked items that I have purchased myself (with some exceptions that were not relevant to my needs). If you want to save time and rely on my recommendations, you can get the products quickly and easily through these links. When choosing these products I paid attention to two things: As best quality as possible and at the same time the best price.

In addition, I provide my treatment program on my website as an example free of charge under the following link:

https://hawloo.eu/treatmentprogram

I hope that this book will help many people find healing and that it will be useful to them on their way to a better life.

THE FIRST CHAPTER:

MY HEALING STORY

THE INVISIBLE PAIN

"THIS IS A MIRACLE" SAID MY DOCTOR
REVERSING HAIR LOSS AND ALOPECIA

When I was a small child, I had small ball-shaped hair loss on my head a few times. I was maybe 9 or 10 years old at the time. The doctor prescribed a cream-like medicine to apply to the bald spots, and it worked. After a few weeks, the bald spots filled with hair again.

When I was 14-15 years old, it happened again. This time it was two spherical bald spots on my head. One spot was right above my forehead and the other behind my ear.

Psychologically, this was very stressful for me because it was noticeable and hard to hide. The doctor again prescribed me a cream-like medicine, but despite some time, my hair did not grow back. At that time, my mother recommended a home remedy for me to apply: black cumin oil.

I applied the black seed oil to the bald spots and it was like a miracle. In a very short time (I can't remember exactly, but I think it was one to two weeks) the bald spots filled with hair again.

I was now 24 years old and had completed my five-year degree in Istanbul, where I traveled to do my study abroad. After that, I started my master's program at Istanbul University. One day I noticed that some places on my beard were going bald. My beard hair started to fall out, and that worried me. Thinking that the spots would grow back soon, I shaved my beard to hide the bald spots. However, the bald spots became more and more, and the worst part was that my eyebrows and eyelashes were also thinning. At the same time, I suffered from extraordinary hair loss that could not be stopped. At the beginning, I applied a liquid remedy that I got at a pharmacy, and I was confident that everything would soon grow back.

But once, when I was in the shower, the drain filled with my hair so much that hardly any water ran through. My hands were full of hair that had fallen out. This was really horrible feeling.

I was losing my hair, but I couldn't do anything about it. Psychologically, this had put a lot of stress on me and it is hard to put the situation into words. I was living in a dorm at the time and on the one hand I didn't want to appear weak in front of my friends, but on the other hand I was devastated inside.

There was only one thing I could do, and that was to cling to my faith and turn to the One Who has everything in His hands. I realized that I am not the owner of anything that seems to be mine. I saw myself as merely the temporary owner of everything given to me, especially my hair. If this hair really belonged to me, I would not want to give it away. If my hair came from my parents, they would not take my hair away from me either. Because my mother was probably even sadder than I was. So it was another being who had given me my hair, and it was this being, in turn, who had taken my hair away from me again.

In the days when I lost more and more hair, I was still confident and thought that my hair would grow back soon. Up to three years, I hoped that my hair would grow back within three months at the latest. From the third year, I hoped that my hair would return within three to six months. But I had never given up hope.

When the bald spots on my head could no longer be hidden, I got myself a cap. I still remember how my mother and grandma burst into tears when they first saw me with the bald spots on my head. I tried to calm them down and explained that it wasn't that bad and that my hair would grow back soon. Then my mother came up with the idea of shaving my head completely to be less noticeable. I did not have to think twice about that.

But as my eyebrows and eyelashes also thinned, it was harder and harder to hide my disease. At some point it was no longer possible to hide it. In addition, I suddenly got many pimples on my face and my nails were no longer healthy. They were partially broken and had white stripes.

I didn't want to socialize with other people anymore until my hair grew back. I thought it would be best to isolate myself from social life for a few months and wait for my hair to grow back.

My parents wanted to take me with them to Germany to have me treated there. Actually, I didn't want to interrupt my studies in Turkey, but on the other hand, I also wanted to avoid that my environment saw me with my new appearance. Therefore, I decided to go to Germany at least for a few weeks.

In Germany, I started an inpatient therapy in a hospital. This was the first professional medical treatment for my hair loss.

The disease was called Alopecia Areata, which means circular hair loss.

When we asked about the cause of this disease, we always got about the same answer:

The exact cause of Alopecia Areata is not fully understood. However, it is believed to be an autoimmune disease in which the immune system incorrectly attacks the hair follicles. There are also some factors that can increase the risk of Alopecia Areata, including genetic predisposition, stress, infections and other autoimmune diseases. However, Alopecia Areata occurs in many people with no known cause.

So no one knew the exact cause. It could be biological, genetic, psychological or metaphysical. The idea that there could be a metaphysical reason behind it is not scientifically proven, but it is my personal conviction.

It is precisely this phenomenon of ignorance that makes this disease so interesting. The answer to the question of "when will I be healthy again" is just as interesting: You don't know. Maybe in a month. Maybe in several months. Maybe in a year or in fact in several years. Perhaps even in 15 years. Or maybe not at all.

Back to where we started. When I arrived in Germany, they immediately started treating me with cortisone infusions at the hospital to stop and counteract the hair loss. I received infusions twice a day for three days. After that, a total of 3 shots were to be given at intervals of 4 weeks each. The doctor's letter further stated the following, "We recommend continuing topical therapy with a corticosteroid solution."

Here is a section from my doctor's letter (I left out some person-specific parts for privacy reasons):

Diagnose(n):   1. Kortikosteroid-Stoßtherapie bei Alopezia areata totalis (ICD10:L63.9)

Aktuelle Anamnese und Befund:
Der Patient stellte sich stationär vor zur 1. Kortikosteroid- Stoßtherapie bei Alopecia areata. Er berichtete, dass bei ihm seit ca. 3 Monaten ein Haarausfall bestehe. Dieser hätte zunächst im Bartbereich begonne. Seit ca. 3 Wochen bestehe auch ein Haarausfall im Bereich des Kapillitiums und am restlichen Körper. Eine Therapie sei bisher mit Beta Galen Lotio durchgeführt worden, wobei sich keine Besserung zeigte. Eine familiäre Vorbelastung oder eine atopische Diathese liegen nicht vor. Abhängigkeiten sowie Allergien werden verneint.
Bei der klinischen Inspektion zeigten sich am Kapillitium, im Bartbereich sowie an der restlichen Körperbehaarung multiple etwa 3 cm große haarlose Areale mit randständigen Flaumhaaren. Die Kopfhaut war reizlos. Im Randbereich waren die Haare leicht epilierbar. Im Bereich der Augenbrauen war normaler Haarwuchs vorhanden.
Die stationäre Aufnahme erfolgte aufgrund einer progredienten dermatologischen Erkrankung und der Notwendigkeit einer intermittierenden intravenösen Therapie. die aufgrund regelmäßiger Kontrollen von Vitalparametern und Blutzucker im Rahmen eines stationären Aufenthaltes durchgeführt werden musste.

Therapie und Verlauf:
Über drei Tage behandelten wir mit Solu Decortin H 250 mg intravenös zweimal täglich. Flankierend verabreichten wir Pantoprazol 40 mg als Magenschutz, Ampho Moronal Suspension zur Candidaprophylaxe und Calcilac Kautabletten als Osteoporoseschutz. Zusätzlich behandelten wir topisch mit Karison Crinale Lösung. Es erfolgten regelmäßige Kontrollen der Vitalparameter und des Blutzuckers. Diese zeigten sich normwertig. Vor Einleitung der Therapie wurde über die möglichen Risiken (wie beispielsweise Hüftkopfnekrose, Blutzucker- und Blutdruckentgleisungen, Unruhe und Schlafstörungen, etc.) ausführlich aufgeklärt.

Procedere und epikritische Bewertung:
Wir entlassen den Patienten in Ihre ambulante Weiterbetreuung. Der Patient wird die nächsten Behandlungen in der Türkei durchführen lassen. Es sollten insgesamt 3 Stöße im Abstand von jeweils 4 Wochen erfolgen. Wir empfehlen die topische Therapie mit einer Kortikosteroidlösung fortzuführen.

After this treatment, I returned to Turkey without noticing any positive developments.

In Istanbul we found a doctor who gave me the infusions - as recommended. Unfortunately, there were no positive effects.

I had lost all my hair, eyebrows, eyelashes and body hair, so that after a total of five to six months all my hair had completely fallen out.

The new name of my disease was: Alopecia Areata Totalis or Alopecia Universalis, which means in short: All hair is lost.

I looked like someone who had gone through chemotherapy. Many people first thought that I had cancer. Many of my acquaintances had not recognized me anymore. It was a very difficult time that I cannot put into words. I did not want to have to give explanations to my acquaintances, so I did not want to meet them at all. The friends and relatives who saw me like this for the first time were shocked. I still can't forget their facial expressions at the time. Some couldn't hold back their tears, some were pale in their faces. And I was the one who tried to comfort them, even though I was the sick one.

Since the beginning of this disease, I had such great psychological pain that I no longer had any desire to live. At that time, I would have preferred to die than to continue living. This inner pain was present almost continuously for four to five years. But you couldn't notice it from the outside unless I talked about it. But I had no desire to do that. Be that as it may, I was not allowed to put an end to my life, since this was forbidden above all by my religion. So suicide was never an option from the beginning. I had to fight. Because I had many reasons for it.

REASONS FOR MY FIGHT
FOR HEALING

1ST REASON: FAITH

According to my faith, this disease was given to me by my Creator. So it did not hit me by chance. I have always believed that the Almighty Creator is not evil and that there must be a good purpose behind my illness. Therefore, I was not allowed to complain or rebel against Him. If He decided that I should get this disease, then it was better for me to get it than not. I thought a lot, but I didn't have a clear answer as to why I was tested with this disease. But now, as I write these lines, I think I know the answer. At least partially.

It is important for me to emphasize that I do not want to exclude with my statements that my illness could have biological, genetic, psychological or other causes. I

t could well be that there are such causes, even though no one in our extended family, neither on my father's nor mother's side, has ever been affected by this disease and nothing of the kind is known about our ancestors. There are certainly "natural" causes for my illness, even if we and the doctors do not know them. However, I still firmly believe that all diseases are given by a Creator whose mercy is infinite, and that these causes are ultimately created by Him and do not arise by chance.

2ND REASON: HOPE

I was 100% sure that there was a cure for my disease as there is for all diseases. However, I had to seek and find this cure. But how could I be so sure I relied on the statements of the Prophet (peace and blessings upon Him); whatever disease the Owner of the universe sent down, He also sent down its cure.[1] This statement was an absolute motivation for me. After 4-5 years, when I was healed and got my hair back, my aunt Esma said the following to me on the phone:

"Selim, I am amazed at how you have persevered for so many years with the same motivation, always seeking and starting a new therapy after each failure. I know so many people with the same disease as you, but they gave up after one or two years at the latest and just accepted the disease." My response to that was:

"Auntie, I might have given up long ago, but I knew there was a cure for my illness. (Then I quoted to her the above statement of my prophet.) I just had to find it, and that's why I never gave up."

3RD REASON: NEARNESS

I knew that the healing could not come from a doctor or a medicine. They could only be an occasion for my healing. The healing comes solely from the Lord of the Worlds. If He wanted to, He could give me the healing without any occasion. It would not be difficult for Him to do so. However, He has laid down as a law in this world that all processes and developments are to be traced back to some reason. But when extraordinary results occur without any cause, that is, when the Legislator goes beyond His own laws, we call it a miracle. Since I was aware of this, that everything is in the hand and decision of the Almighty, I turned to Him primarily for my health since my hair loss had started. This led me to have and need to have a "close contact" with my Lord. By "close contact" I mean that I spent almost all of my time making supplications. Almost every moment I begged my Lord, whose mercy is infinite, to deliver me from this

---

[1] Buhârî, Tıbb 1, Ebu Dâvud, Tıbb 1, (3855); Tirmizî, Tıbb 2, (2039); İbnu Mâce, Tıbb 1, (3436).

illness. These prayers calmed the fire in me the most.

I knew that my illness and all illnesses were "guests" sent by Creator. I had to patiently "host" these "guests" according to God's pleasure until they left. Therefore, I was constantly in "supplication mode." This attitude and mindset was perhaps one of the purposes why this disease was given to me, namely so that I could get closer to Him. If He had not given me this disease, I might have forgotten Him.

But supplication has two kinds: one with words (speech supplication) and the other with actions (actional supplication). The supplications I expressed with my mouth, my inner voices or with my feelings and tears belonged to the first kind. On the other hand, my search and research for healing, my visits to doctors, the therapies I used, and the medications I took were the second kind of supplication. In short, the fact that I fought for my healing was at the same time a directed supplication to the One to whom everything belongs. The result of (supplication) prayer is closeness to the Lord of the Worlds. Perhaps this illness was given to me only so that I would make these supplications and worship Him, because supplication alone is worship.

ADVANTAGES THAT CAME WITH MY DISEASE

During the times when I was ill, I was aware of some benefits despite the difficulty of my illness. However, after my recovery, I became aware of many more benefits, and I am still discovering more. Aside from the benefits I mentioned below, there are many more that I will not list here, as it is beyond the scope of this book. In fact, I could possibly write a stand-alone book on the benefits that my disease brought alone. So in the following are the benefits that I became aware of, and I'm sure I didn't discover all the benefits yet. Someday I may uncover the other benefits that are unknown to me.

1st Advantage: A special closeness

Even if the All-Merciful One gave me this disease just so that I could come closer to Him and worship Him, all the sorrow and pain I experienced and all my efforts (in terms of money and energy) were worth it. Because getting closer to Him is a price that precedes everything. But please don't misunderstand me: I would never have willingly accepted this illness and these difficult times, nor would I ever wish for the same or anything similar. Nor can I claim that I have always maintained or will maintain this closeness to Him. All I am saying is that this illness has brought me closer to my Lord and that this has probably been the greatest benefit of all.

2nd Advantage: Sociological

Before I got sick with this disease, I had not that much empathy for sick and disabled people. I simply ignored them. I also didn't have any idea how to deal with such people. However, this illness made me become a more sensitive person. I have better understood the psyche of such people and can now imagine that they may be feeling a lot of pain inside, even if they do not show it outwardly. Therefore, one should definitely take this into account and behave appropriately. So I have learned through my own experience how to behave towards people with disabilities or illnesses. This was a valuable lesson that I was able to learn because of my illness.

Before I get to the third advantage, I want to talk about what I learned here:

Empty hope:

I have heard many well-intentioned words of comfort, but unfortunately they were unnecessary. For example, an acquaintance told me that hair is so unimportant that you can't even sell it. A comparable example would be to say to a person in a wheelchair: "Hey, legs are not important at all. If you wanted to sell them, you couldn't even get money off them." Many men without hair also tried to give me comfort by telling me they were bald too. The point, however, was that not only did I have no hair on my head, I had no eyebrows, eyelashes or beard. So these attempts were well-intentioned, but unfortunately unnecessary.

Resistance:

I'll never forget the moment a friend told me to my face, "Just accept that you don't have hair anymore." If I had taken him seriously, I would have been devastated. I was 24 years old at the time, and the idea of having to live with the way I looked then for the rest of my life almost killed me. Fortunately, I didn't take his advice and never gave up. You should never tell a person with a disease to give up. Instead, you should encourage her and support her in never giving up.

Be realistic:

Of course, there were also many people who simply ignored my illness and acted as if I were completely normal. Yes, you can do that, but I think that this is not the best behavior. Once, when I told an acquaintance about my disease, he replied, as if he hadn't noticed, "What, you don't have hair?" That didn't make things any better, and it really didn't have to. Because it made me feel kind of made fun of.

Conduct open communication:

I found people who talked openly and confidently with me about my illness the best. Some asked profoundly if the disease was bothering me, while others were concerned about me and asked how the therapy was going. Some also said that I looked charismatic, while my friend Tural in London even advised me that it would be the best time for me to get married because a woman who accepts me like that would always accept me. I especially liked the fact that he didn't embellish or minimize my unusual looks, and he didn't think I was stupid either. This advice was really good, but I still didn't follow it.

3RD ADVANTAGE: EXPERTISE

Due to my illness, I have gained a lot of knowledge in the health industry, especially in the field of nutrition and hair growth. I even learned about the bioenergy therapy. In one of the following chapters I will go into more detail concering this topic. And also to mention I have expanded my knowledge in psychology and education.

4TH ADVANTAGE: COACHING

With my expertise, I have been able to help many people around me and ensure that they lead a much healthier and successful life. In addition, I could or can support and coach them psychologically, which really fulfills me in my life.

5TH ADVANTAGE: PATIENCE

I learned that I should never be too confident. Before my illness, I never imagined that I would ever lose my hair because it was very full and strong. Even the people around me told me that I would never lose my hair.

But when I lost my hair, it was an important lesson for me. I realized that everything is in the hands of the Owner of the Universe. He can give when and what He wants; He can take away when and what He wants. I experienced this firsthand. The decision and power are his alone. He does not have to do anything, but he can. Therefore, I do not have the right to complain, but should always be grateful.

6TH ADVANTAGE: NEW ACQUAINTANCES

Just as I gained new knowledge through this disease, I also met many interesting people, some of whom became my best friends. One of them was Ziya Pasha, a great brother and true friend for this and another life. I was introduced to him because some useful connections and contacts by another very good friend of mine, Mehmet Karadeniz. If I had not had this disease, I might never have met these wonderful people.

7TH ADVANTAGE: CHARACTER

Since I had attached a lot of importance to my appearance. Before my illness, I thought that everyone paid attention to my appearance. Of course, appearance is not unimportant, but I had overrated the outer appearance far too much.

However, after I got this disease, I noticed that none of my friends, acquaintances or relatives turned away from me. Although my appearance had completely changed, their attitude and behavior towards me remained unchanged.

Even with new people who saw me for the first time, their behavior was almost always normal. But honestly, there were also cases when I noticed that I was perceived differently by some people. Just these individual cases hurt me very much, although they were actually only individual cases.

However, on the whole, I understood that what really matters is the character and the inside, not the outside. Now I try to attach only as much importance to the appearance as it is worth.

8TH ADVANTAGE: WISDOM

I hope that I will also help millions of people with this book, both in my lifetime and after. I believe that many people will see themselves reflected in my life and they may draw some lessons for themselves from my life. For many, I hope this book will be a comfort. It would fulfill me if through this book they would avoid the mistakes I made and find a shortcut to their goal or healing. That alone would be something that no price can buy.

9TH ADVANTAGE: TRANSFORMATION

In addition, I may also make financial gains from the book if it becomes popular and sells. So my illness could become a source of money.

Imagine, all these benefits would not be there if I had not suffered from this disease, specifically my hair loss.

What do you think now? Were all my experienced sorrows, tears, pains, costs, etc. not worth it to gain these benefits?

For me, the answer is quite clear.

Now you can think about what benefits you could take from your illness to turn it into something positive!

25

MY JOURNEY THROUGH THE THERAPIES

Before writing this book, I was aware that I had been through many different therapies, but it wasn't until I wrote them down that I realized how numerous they actually were.

1) CORTISONE TREATMENT

As already mentioned, I started cortisone therapy in Germany and then continued it in Istanbul. Unfortunately, however, it did not bring any success.

2) OZONE THERAPY

As a result, I started ozone therapy in Istanbul. Ozone therapy is an alternative form of therapy that uses ozone ($O3$) as a therapeutic agent. Ozone is a form of oxygen that contains three oxygen atoms, as opposed to the two atoms in normal oxygen ($O2$).

The benefits of ozone therapy are controversial and depend on the type of application and the specific disease for which it is used. Some possible benefits of ozone therapy are:

1. Reduction of pain and inflammation: Ozone is believed to have anti-inflammatory effects and can reduce pain.

2. Improving blood circulation: Ozone is believed to improve blood circulation, thereby promoting the growth of new tissues and cells.

3. Strengthening the immune system: Ozone is believed to strengthen the immune system, thereby reducing the risk of infections.

4. Improving oxygen uptake: Ozone is believed to improve the absorption of oxygen into the blood, thereby increasing physical performance.

It is important to note that ozone therapy is a controversial form of therapy and there is not enough scientific evidence to support most of its claimed benefits. Some experts even warn of possible risks and side effects of ozone therapy, including damage to the lungs and other organs.

I don't remember it that well, but I think I had one to two sessions a week at that time, for a couple months.

3) ACUPUNCTURE

After I could not achieve any success with ozone therapy, I started my acupuncture treatment in Istanbul.

Acupuncture is a traditional Chinese healing method that uses fine needles in specific areas of the body to relieve pain, relax the body, and activate the body's own healing system. Possible benefits of acupuncture include pain relief, relaxation, improvement of sleep quality, treatment of chronic diseases, and improvement of physical functions. Although there is insufficient scientific evidence to back most of these benefits up, acupuncture can help when performed by an experienced acupuncturist.

After I started these two therapies, it was with me that after about a month on my head area some hair roots were visible. There were maybe 10 - 15 pieces of 1 - 2mm long thin hairs. I was so happy and thought to myself that now it will go up and all my hair will come back in a few months. That is why I had continued with the treatment. However, although these spots had increased a bit, they had not started to grow. They had unfortunately remained like that. At some point, due to lack of progress and high costs, I had decided to stop the treatment.

4) OINTMENTS, SHAMPOOS AND VARIOUS TEAS

During the time of ozone and acupuncture therapy, I was at the same time looking for other treatments in case they didn't work out. Because I carried the inner pain with me throughout and wanted to get rid of it immediately. As quickly as possible. My pain was so immense that if I had seen any therapy that had the slightest chance of recovery, I didn't want to miss it. Because you could never know, maybe that therapy could be the reason for my recovery.

With regard to this, I had dealt a lot with natural healing methods. I wanted to believe all those who had promised a recovery for my illness. So I ordered various ointments and teas. If I were to list here one by one all the natural healing products I have used in terms of ointments, shampoos, creams and teas, it would take a very long time.

The interesting thing was that almost all suppliers of these natural healing products were almost 100% sure that I would find the cure with their products. Unfortunately, it was not the case at that time. With these statements I am not trying to claim that they were scammers. I can't know that and I would never claim something like that. But one thing was clear, the real cause of my recovery were not these natural healing products.

In this regard, I would like to say that the application of these natural healing products was by no means easy.

Some I had to apply and wait for certain time. Others I had to leave applied even overnight, which was the most challenging part for me.

For example, I remember an ointment that had a dark brown color and had stunk quite badly. The stench was so intense that when I applied it, the whole room and almost my entire dorm (I am not exaggerating) had stunk of wood grill. It stunk as if you had lit wood and coal in our room.

I would like to tell you now about my (in retrospect) funny experience. Since it stunk so badly, I always went into a empty room after I had applied the ointment to my scalp. All of a sudden I noticed that a commotion had broken out in my home. Some people in charge were going up and down the stairs talking about how there was a fire in the building. That's when I knew right away what the deal was. Namely, the supposed fire I was looking for was on my head.

At that time I did not find it funny at all, but now that I write these lines, I must inevitably blurt out.

Back then, I had felt very uncomfortable admitting that the strange smell that had erupted in the dorm was from my ointment and not from a fire. But I finally admitted it. However, they did not believe me and insisted that it must be a fire. I had then said nothing more and they finally realized on their own that I was telling the truth.

However, the smell of the ointment was very persistent and did not disappear even when I opened the window or aired the room. I don't remember exactly how long I had to endure this, but I think it was a few months.

In addition to the ointment, I had also tried various teas, some were good and others less so. I had gone through this for years and kept ordering new teas, but unfortunately, I had not noticed any positive effect.

Before I forget, I also want to mention that for a long time I had been swallowing a clove of garlic every night before bed. I had read somewhere that it was supposed to boost either hair growth or the immune system. I also found that very difficult, but despite that I had to try it.

5) BIOENERGY THERAPY

I learned from my Azarbaijani friend named Mikail, who studied at my university, that he had become a bioenergy therapist and later even opened his own practice. I told him about my illness and he offered to treat me with bioenergy free of charge.

Bioenergy therapy is an alternative form of therapy based on the theory that the human body has an energy system that can be affected by blockages and disharmonies that can lead to physical and emotional problems. The therapy aims to release these blockages and harmonize the energy system to promote healing and well-being. Bioenergy therapy originated in traditional Chinese medicine and has evolved over time to include a variety of techniques such as tapping, breathing exercises, bodywork and meditation.

Without doing any deeper research, I immediately had my friend treat me because I believed that blockages in my energy system could be the cause of my illness. He treated me once or twice a week and I received a total of twelve sessions.

I was impressed by this therapy and felt like I was in a new world. Although I did not notice any outward difference, I wanted to delve into this and asked my friend to teach me this therapy. He did it and I also read various books on it. Eventually, I was able to feel and control the physical bioenergy of another in my hand, and I started doing therapy for other people.

In the end, however, I must confess that this therapy did not lead to the healing of my illness. Nevertheless, I believe that my blockages in my energy system were released and that this process was by no means in vain and unnecessary.

6) HELLINGER THERAPY

I don't remember where I heard about it, but somewhere I had heard about a therapy called Hellinger therapy. There was a center for it in an elite neighborhood of Istanbul. I had called and described my illness. They said that in my case it could very well be a deep problem anchored in my subconscious. Without knowing what kind of therapy it even was, I wanted to try it. I had only one session, which had cost me a lot, and just for that reason it was more than enough for me. Much later, when I learned what the "therapy" actually was, I realized that it was not for me at all.

Hellinger therapy is a form of systemic therapy developed by German psychotherapist Bert Hellinger. It aims to bring about profound changes in relationships and family systems by identifying the hidden patterns and dynamics that influence behavior and relationships.

Hellinger therapy works with the concepts of order and disorder in family and relationship systems. It assumes that every family has its own order, which is shaped by behavioral patterns and entanglements that stem from the past. If these patterns and entanglements are not resolved, problems can arise in relationships and behavior.

Hellinger therapy uses a variety of techniques, including

family constellations, in which participants symbolically represent their relationships and family structures to identify hidden patterns and entanglements. The therapy aims to resolve these patterns and entanglements and restore order in the system to allow for change and healing.

It is important to note that Hellinger therapy is a controversial form of therapy and there is not enough scientific evidence of its effectiveness. I myself had not noticed any real effectiveness in terms of my recovery, except that I felt psychologically relieved at the time.

7) METAPHYSICAL TREATMENTS

This part is about a topic that has an important position according to my beliefs. It is the concept of the "evil eye," which is common in many cultures around the world. It refers to the idea that someone can affect or spoil other people or objects through negative thoughts or looks. This is often done unintentionally out of envy, ill will, or jealousy.

The "evil eye" is often associated with certain symptoms such as illness, bad luck or bad fortune. To combat it, various cultures use protective measures such as amulets, talismans or ritual acts.

It should be noted that the concept of the evil eye is subjective and is not recognized by the scientific community. There is no scientific evidence for the effectiveness of measures to protect against the evil eye or for the existence of the evil eye as a real phenomenon. However, it is a part of folklore, traditions and belief systems that play an important role for many people.

Because the "evil eye" could be a possible reason for my illness, I wanted to exclude all probabilities. Because it could be indeed that one or more djinn or as mentioned the evil eye was the reason for a disease.

By inquiries in my circle of acquaintances I had found some supposed experts in the field of metaphysics and had asked them whether my illness possibly had a metaphysical background. Many of them had confirmed to me that this was possible. They had offered me their help, which I accepted and paid. Then the treatment began and they gave me an inscribed muska to carry with me at all times.

For years I wore this muska until one day I lost it or decided not to wear it anymore. However, I did not notice any signs of improvement in my disease related to this treatment. Nevertheless, I am convinced that the cure of some diseases can only be metaphysical.

8) LOCAL CORTICOSTEROIDS AND MICANOL 1 %.

After about a year since the beginning of my illness, I dropped out of my master's program at Istanbul University and moved near Frankfurt. There I wanted to start a new master's program at Goethe University.

After spending a year in Turkey trying out many treatment methods of the Orient, it was now time to turn back to Western medicine.

I had researched and went directly to a university clinic whose name I do not want to mention. There they prescribed me a corticosteroid cream and a liquid medication called Micanol 1% to apply. I was almost sure that it wouldn't do any good and that I would lose a lot of time for nothing, but I still followed the prescribed therapy. I think that my doctor was also almost sure that this medicine would not do anything, but still he prescribed it to me. It seemed to me, and probably was, that he didn't care about my recovery. For me, every single day was another pain, but he could say with no worries, "Apply this ointment and come back after two months."

I went out. With sadness and some anger.

9) SECOND INPATIENT CORTISONE THERAPY

After my doctors understood that the local corticosteroids and Micanol 1% would not help me, they decided to give me the so-called steroid pulse therapy as an inpatient in the hospital three days a month for six months. This involved giving me one or more doses of cortisone infusion daily. Psychologically, these days were very stressful for me. During this inpatient treatment I was almost always alone, both on the way there and back and during my stay. I did not want to disclose my treatment to those around me. Only a dear, loyal friend and big brother of mine, Toprak abi, a former top journalist, came to visit me during these times and brought me delicious food against my will.

Here are the sections from my doctor's letters on this (for privacy reasons, I've cut away some person-specific parts):

Sehr geehrte Frau Kollegin, sehr geehrter Herr Kollege,

wir berichten über Ihren o.g. Patienten, der sich vom 05.02.2016 bis zum 08.02.2016 zur Behandlung bei Alopecia universalis in unserer stationären Behandlung (Station 28-1) befand.

Hauptdiagnose

L63.1   Alopecia universalis

Anamnese

Die stationäre Aufnahme des Patienten erfolgt zur Steroid-Pulstherapie bei Alopecia universalis. Der Patient berichtet über seit 2014 zunehmenden Haarausfall, initial kreisrund am Bart. Im Verlauf auch Kopfhaut und Schambereich betroffen. Seit Februar 2015 vollständiger Haarverlust am gesamten Integument. Diverse Vortherapien darunter eine Steroid-Pulstherapie 10/2014, sowie lokale Kortikosteroide und Micanol 1% ohne Befundsverbesserung.

Pat.: Selim Dursun, Geb.Dat.: 06.04.1990, M

FA: leer bezüglich Haut

Dermatologischer Befund

Gesamter Haarverlust des Integuments, Haarfollikel erhalten.

Labor

Bezeichnung	Ref.-Bereich	Einheit	5.2.16 19:45
CRP im Serum	<0,50	mg/dl	0,11
Natrium im Serum	135 - 145	mmol/l	141
Kalium im Serum	3,6 - 4,8	mmol/l	4.61
Kreatinin im Serum	0,7 - 1,2	mg/dl	0.76
Glucose im Serum	74 - 106	mg/dl	**127**
GPT im Serum	<50	U/l	16
MDRD-Formel		ml/min/ 1,73 m2	>120.0
CKD-Epi	77 - 179	ml/min/ 1,73 m2	>120.0
Leukozyten im BB	4,0 - 10,4	/ nl	10.11
Erythrozyten im BB	4,54 - 5,77	/ pl	5.06
HB im BB	13.5 - 17.5	g/dl	15.5
Hämatokrit im BB	39.6 - 50.6	%	45.1
MCH im BB	27.6 - 32.6	pg	30.6
MCHC im BB	32.8 - 36.6	g/dl	34.4
MCV im BB	80.0 - 95.5	fl	68.1
Thrombozyten im BB	163 - 337	/ nl	257
RDW	12.1 - 14.8	%	13.4
Basophile abs.	0,01 - 0,08	/ nl	0.01
Eosinophile abs.	0,04 - 0,54	/ nl	0.01
Lymphozyten abs.	1,32 - 3,57	/ nl	**0.40**
Monozyten abs.	0,3 - 0,82	/ nl	**0.05**
Neutrophile abs.	1,78 - 5,36	/ nl	**9.64**
Basophile proz.	0,2 - 1,2	%	**0.10**
Eosinophile proz.	0,8 - 7,0	%	**0.10**
Lymphozyten proz.	21,8 - 53,1	%	**4.0**
Monozyten proz.	5,3 - 12,2	%	**0.50**
Neutrophile proz.	34 - 67,9	%	**95.30**
unreife Granulozyten absolut		/ nl	0.03
unreife Granulozyten prozentual		%	0.30

Therapie und Verlauf

Die stationäre Aufnahme des Patienten erfolgte zur intravenösen Steroidpulstherapie mit 500 mg Methylprednisolon für 3 Tage unter Kontrolle der Blutdruck- und Blutzuckerwerte zur Behandlung der Alopecia universalis.

Die Steroidpulstherapie wurde problemlos vertragen. Die Nachbeobachtung zeigte sich problemlos, sodass wir den Patienten am 08.02.2016 in die ambulante Behandlung entlassen konnten.

Letzte Medikation

Medikament	Dosisschema ggf. körpermaßbezogen
Pantozol 40	1-0-0-0 (Stück)
Unizink 50 mg	50-0-0-0 (mg)

Weiteres Vorgehen

Dermatologischer Arztbrief, gedruckt am 08.02.2016 11:04

Pat. Selim Dursun Geb.Dat. 06.04.1990, M

Wir empfehlen die Fortsetzung der Einnahme von Pantozol 40 1-0-0 für weitere 3 Tage. Unizink sollte bis auf weiteres 1x täglich eingenommen werden.
Ein Termin zur Verlaufskontrolle und Planung des nächsten Steroidpulses wurde für Freitag 04.03.16 um 10.00 Uhr in unserer Hochschulambulanz (H28 3 Stock) vereinbart.

Dieser vorläufige Brief für die weiterbetreuenden Ärzte wird dem Patienten mit Kenntnisstand zum Entlassungszeitpunkt ausgehändigt. Ein endgültiger Arztbrief folgt nach Eingang aller evtl. noch ausstehenden Befunde. Dies kann 2-3 Wochen in Anspruch nehmen.

Für Rückfragen stehen wir gerne zur Verfügung und verbleiben

mit freundlichen kollegialen Grüßen

Here are sections from another doctor's letter:

Vorläufiger Arztbrief

Selim Dursun, geb. 06.04.1990

Sehr geehrte Frau Kollegin, sehr geehrter Herr Kollege,

wir berichten über Ihren o.g. Patienten, der sich vom 10.03.2016 bis zum 12.03.2016 zur Behandlung bei Alopecia universalis in unserer stationären Behandlung (Station 28-1) befand.

Hauptdiagnose

L63.1   **Alopecia areata totalis**

Anamnese

Die stationäre Aufnahme des Patienten erfolgt zur zweiten Steroid-Pulstherapie bei Alopecia areata totalis.
Der Patient berichtet über seit 2014 zunehmenden Haarausfall, initial kreisrund am Bart. Im Verlauf auch Kopfhaut und Schambereich betroffen. Seit Februar 2015 vollständiger Haarverlust am gesamten Integument. Diverse Vortherapien darunter eine Steroid-Pulstherapie 10/2014, der aber nach einmaliger Gabe abgebrochen wurde, sowie lokale Kortikosteroide und Micanol 1% ohne Befundsverbesserung. Im Februar diesen Jahres wurde erneut eine Steroidstoßtherapie initiiert. Aktuell erfolgt die Aufnahme zum zweiten Zyklus.

Grunderkrankungen: keine

Pat.: Selim Dursun, Geb.Dat.: 08.04.1990, M 2/3

Allergien: keine bekannt
Noxen: Rauchen: Nichtraucher; Alkohol: selten
SA: Student; ledig; keine Kinder
FA: leer bezüglich Haut

Dermatologischer Befund

Gesamter Haarverlust des Integuments, Haarfollikel erhalten.

Labor

Bezeichnung	Ref.-Bereich	Einheit	10.3.18 11:27
CRP im Serum	<0,50	mg/dl	**0.63**
Natrium im Serum	135 - 145	mmol/l	**146**
Kalium im Serum	3,6 - 4,8	mmol/l	4.34
Kreatinin im Serum	0,7 - 1,2	mg/dl	0.90
Harnstoff im Serum	19 - 44	mg/dl	23
Harnsäure im Serum	3,4 - 7,0	mg/dl	**3.2**
Glucose im Serum	74 - 106	mg/dl	**70**
GOT im Serum	<40	U/l	21
GPT im Serum	<50	U/l	12
GGT im Serum	<60	U/l	15
Alk.Phosphat im Serum	40 - 130	U/l	54
MDRD-Formel		ml/min/ 1,73 m2	102.8
CKD-Epi	77 - 179	ml/min/ 1,73 m2	118.3
Leukozyten im BB	4,0 - 10,4	/ nl	7.37
Erythrozyten im BB	4.54 - 5.77	/ pl	5.02
HB im BB	13.5 - 17.5	g/dl	14.8
Hämatokrit im BB	39.5 - 50.6	%	44.9
MCH im BB	27.6 - 32.8	pg	29.5
MCHC im BB	32.8 - 36.6	g/dl	33.0
MCV im BB	80.0 - 95.5	fl	89.4
Thrombozyten im BB	163 - 337	/ nl	279
RDW	12.1 - 14.8	%	13.6
Basophile abs.	0,01 - 0,08	/ nl	0.05
Eosinophile abs.	0,04 - 0,54	/ nl	0.12
Lymphozyten abs.	1.32 - 3,57	/ nl	1.5
Monozyten abs.	0,3 - 0.82	/ nl	0.74
Neutrophile abs.	1,78 - 5,38	/ nl	4.95
Basophile proz.	0,2 - 1,2	%	0.70
Eosinophile proz.	0,8 - 7,0	%	1.60
Lymphozyten proz.	21,8 - 53,1	%	**20.5**
Monozyten proz.	5,3 - 12,2	%	10.0
Neutrophile proz.	34 - 67,9	%	67.20
unreife Granulozyten absolut		/ nl	0.01
unreife Granulozyten prozentual		%	0.10

Therapie und Verlauf

Die stationäre Aufnahme des Patienten erfolgte zur intravenösen Steroidpulstherapie mit 500 mg Methylprednisolon für 3 Tage unter Kontrolle der Blutdruck- und Blutzuckerwerte zur Behandlung der Alopecia universalis.

Die Steroidpulstherapie wurde problemlos vertragen. Die Nachbeobachtung zeigte sich problemlos, sodass wir

Dermatologischer Arztbrief, gedruckt am 11.03.2018 16:40

Pat.: Selim Dursun, Geb.Dat.: **06.04.1990**, M   3/3

den Patienten am 12.03.2016 in die ambulante Behandlung entlassen konnten.

Letzte Medikation

Medikament	Dosisschema ggf. körpermaßbezogen
Pantozol 40	1-0-0-0 (Stück)
Unizink 50 mg	50-0-0-0 (mg)

Weiteres Vorgehen

Wir empfehlen die Fortsetzung der Einnahme von Pantozol 40 1-0-0 für weitere 3 Tage. Unizink sollte bis auf weiteres 1x täglich eingenommen werden
Ein Termin zur 3. Steroidpulstherapie wurde am Mittwoch, den 06.04.2016 vereinbart. Der Patient sollte sich um 07:00 Uhr morgens beim Aufnahmemanagement ███████████████████████ melden.

Dieser vorläufige Brief für die weiterbetreuenden Ärzte wird dem Patienten mit Kenntnisstand zum Entlassungszeitpunkt ausgehändigt. Ein endgültiger Arztbrief folgt nach Eingang aller evtl. noch ausstehenden Befunde. Dies kann 2-3 Wochen in Anspruch nehmen.

Für Rückfragen stehen wir gerne zur Verfügung und verbleiben

mit freundlichen kollegialen Grüßen

And here is the last doctor's letter from the same hospital regarding her treatment:

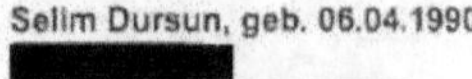

Selim Dursun, geb. 06.04.1990

Sehr geehrte Frau Kollegin, sehr geehrter Herr Kollege,

wir berichten über Ihren o.g. Patienten, der sich vom 25.07.2016 bis zum 27.07.2016 zur Steroidpulstherapie bei Alopecia areata universalis in unserer stationären Behandlung (Station 28-2) befand.

Hauptdiagnose

L63.8   **Alopecia areata universalis**

     Aktuell: 6. Steroidpulstherapie

Anamnese

Die stationäre Aufnahme des Patienten erfolgt zur 6. Steroidpulstherapie bei Alopecia areata universalis. Der Patient berichtet über seit 2014 zunehmenden Haarausfall, initial kreisrund am Bart. Im Verlauf auch Kopfhaut und Schambereich betroffen. Seit Februar 2015 vollständiger Haarverlust am gesamten Integument. Diverse Vortherapien darunter eine Steroidpulstherapie 10/2014, die aber nach einmaliger Gabe abgebrochen wurde, sowie lokale Kortikosteroide und Micanol 1% ohne Befundverbesserung. Im Februar 2016 wurde erneut eine Steroidstoßtherapie initiiert. Die letzten fünf Zyklen wurden problemlos vertragen. Es zeigen sich vereinzelte neue Haare im Bart-, sowie Schambereich.

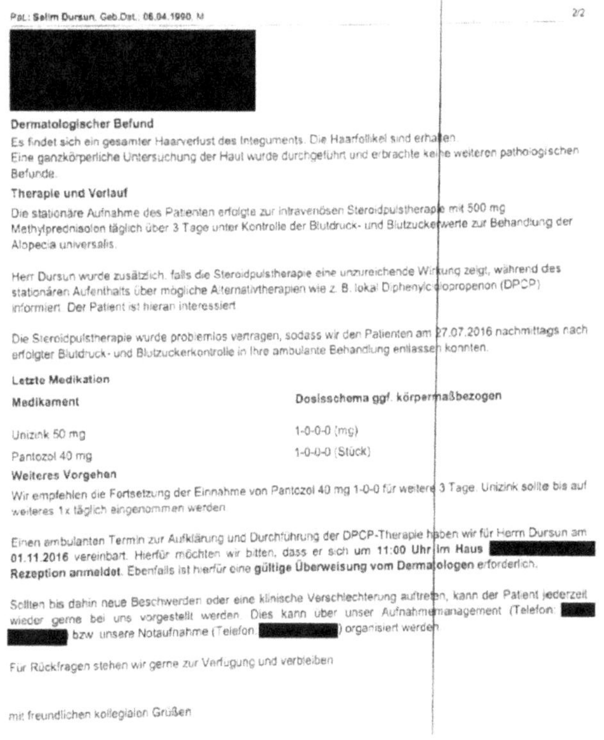

Pat.: Salim Dursun, Geb.Dat.: 06.04.1990, M   2/2

Dermatologischer Befund

Es findet sich ein gesamter Haarverlust des Integuments. Die Haarfollikel sind erhalten.
Eine ganzkörperliche Untersuchung der Haut wurde durchgeführt und erbrachte keine weiteren pathologischen
Befunde.

Therapie und Verlauf

Die stationäre Aufnahme des Patienten erfolgte zur intravenösen Steroidpulstherapie mit 500 mg
Methylprednisolon täglich über 3 Tage unter Kontrolle der Blutdruck- und Blutzuckerwerte zur Behandlung der
Alopecia universalis.

Herr Dursun wurde zusätzlich, falls die Steroidpulstherapie eine unzureichende Wirkung zeigt, während des
stationären Aufenthalts über mögliche Alternativtherapien wie z. B. lokal Diphenylciclopropenon (DPCP)
informiert. Der Patient ist hieran interessiert.

Die Steroidpulstherapie wurde problemlos vertragen, sodass wir den Patienten am 27.07.2016 nachmittags nach
erfolgter Blutdruck- und Blutzuckerkontrolle in Ihre ambulante Behandlung entlassen konnten.

Letzte Medikation

Medikament	Dosisschema ggf. körpermaßbezogen
Unizink 50 mg	1-0-0-0 (mg)
Pantozol 40 mg	1-0-0-0 (Stück)

Weiteres Vorgehen

Wir empfehlen die Fortsetzung der Einnahme von Pantozol 40 mg 1-0-0 für weitere 3 Tage. Unizink sollte bis auf
weiteres 1x täglich eingenommen werden.

Einen ambulanten Termin zur Aufklärung und Durchführung der DPCP-Therapie haben wir für Herrn Dursun am
01.11.2016 vereinbart. Hierfür möchten wir bitten, dass er sich um 11:00 Uhr im Haus ▮▮▮▮
Rezeption anmeldet. Ebenfalls ist hierfür eine gültige Überweisung vom Dermatologen erforderlich.

Sollten bis dahin neue Beschwerden oder eine klinische Verschlechterung auftreten, kann der Patient jederzeit
wieder gerne bei uns vorgestellt werden. Dies kann über unser Aufnahmemanagement (Telefon: ▮▮▮
▮▮▮▮ bzw. unsere Notaufnahme (Telefon: ▮▮▮▮▮) organisiert werden.

Für Rückfragen stehen wir gerne zur Verfügung und verbleiben

mit freundlichen kollegialen Grüßen

10)   DIPHENYLCYCLOPROPENONE (DPCP)

As described in the last doctor's letter, after six months of inpatient
cortisone therapy, which had no effect, the doctors had suggested
the drug Diphenylcyclopropenone (DPCP) to me. Although I was in a
hopeless situation, I accepted the offer. DPCP is a chemical agent
commonly used in the treatment of alopecia areata, an autoimmune
disorder that causes hair loss. It is applied directly to the head and
causes local inflammation, which is supposed to cause the immune

system to not more attack the hair follicle and allow the hair to grow back if treated properly. DPCP is not suitable for all people with alopecia areata and may cause possible side effects, including skin irritation and itching in the treated areas.

My doctor had initially prescribed a low dose of DPCP and recommended that I apply it daily to the bald spots on my head. I was to leave it on for some time (I don't remember exactly, but I think it was about 30 minutes) and then wash it off.

Unfortunately, I had not paid attention at the beginning and thought that I could leave the liquid medicine on the applied areas overnight. I had even applied it to my beard on my face. When I woke up the next morning and looked in the mirror, I got a shock. The areas where I had applied the medicine - my beard, mustache, and head area - were stained a dark brown. It looked like the areas were burned. I tried to wash the areas off with water, but it was too late. Then, when I read the instructions for the medication, I realized that it should only be left on for a short time (as I said, I don't remember exactly how long). I just looked terrible and didn't know how I could go out in public like that. I didn't even know if the discoloration would go away and my skin would recover. Because like I said, it felt like my skin (maybe it really was) was burned.

I had learned my lesson: You should never use a medicine without first carefully reading the instructions.

Well, either way, I had to go out in public and explain, if necessary, that the discoloration of my skin occurred because of a medication. Thank God, after a few weeks my skin had regenerated and the discoloration was gone.

After a month or two, I went back to my doctor. When he saw that the treatment had not had a positive effect, he increased the dose of DPCP a little and sent me away again.

A few months later I came back, but there was still no progress. Nothing at all. So guess what my doctor did next? That's right, he increased the dose even more.

It went on like that, probably for three to six months. The last dose he prescribed me was 2% (if I remember correctly), which also had no effect. [43]

I came back and that was my last meeting with my doctor at this hospital. Why it was the last meeting, I will come to that in the following.

THE TURNING POINT

After the 2% dose of DPCP had no effect, my doctor told me in our last meeting that they could not increase the dose any further. I then asked him:

- I see. What happens now?
- We did everything we could do.
- How? Is there no other therapy option?
- No. There is nothing more we can do for you.

Completely dry! My doctor told me straight to my face, in his professional way, that after lengthy therapies, psychologically stressful hospital stays, long waiting times and high costs, it was all over. Maybe he wanted to express that he had no more hope that I would get well again, but he did not say it. Because if he had done so, he might have questioned his professionalism.

Later I read on the Internet that the probability of recovering from my illness is only 3%.

As a person who had hope with all treatments (except for those few treatments I mentioned) to get well within three months, I ask you:

How do you think I felt at that moment?

Should I now think that I will never get my hair back and live the rest of my life without hair, eyebrows, eyelashes and beard? Should I now accept my disease and resign myself to it, as a friend recommended to me years ago in Istanbul? Should I break down, run out sobbing like a child, Or should I curse my doctor for stringing me along for more than a year with bullshit "treatments" that he didn't even believe in himself? How should I think and act now?

No! None of that entered my head at the time. Not in the least. I had at that moment a quite controversial thought to those mentioned in the previous paragraph. To wit: Interestingly, an unexpected feeling of happiness jumped up in me at that moment.

Yes, that's right. That's actually how it was. Even if you wouldn't believe me. Just to be able to tell you an interesting story here, I didn't make all this up. As strange as it sounds, the moment my doctor had given up hope, I had gotten the hope to get well again. At that moment I had felt the strongest faith that I would be cured all the more despite what my doctor had decided. The reason is this:

At that moment, I immediately thought of the true story of a wise man that I had read years ago. The story was as follows:

The wise man, because of his paralysis on one side of his body, went to the doctor once again after lengthy therapies. His doctor asked him:

- What complaints do you have?
- I have no complaints.

The doctor got a little excited and asked further:

- Then why did you come if you have no complaints?
- I have come because I am trying to follow the laws of my God. Whoever has a disease should seek its cure. I am looking for the cure, but I have no complaint, certainly not to my God.

Thereupon the doctor told him:

- I am sorry, but you can no longer be cured.
- Thank God.
- Why are you suddenly thanking God now?
- Before you told me that I can no longer be healed on your part, I had a little misconception that maybe the doctors and medicines could heal me. But now that you have said it, I have become quite sure again that the healing can only

come from God. All possible causes have now fallen. And He alone is now the only one who can give me the healing apart from these occasions and now I can turn to Him 100%. That was the reason why I thanked Him.

Back to me. Why I suddenly became happy when my doctor told me "That now everything is over" was that I remembered the above real incident. At that moment I thought:

"Now all kinds of occasions have fallen. And only You, my Lord, can give me the cure. And only to You do I turn."

As these thoughts passed through my mind, I felt so strong and so relieved that I find it hard to put into words. I can still remember quite well with what joy I had set out on the way home. Inwardly I said firmly:

"I know you will heal me. I know it."

But do you know why I was so sure?

Because I had experience. No matter what I had asked of my Lord, as long as I asked it with firm conviction and persistence, He had given it to me. And also in this case, He enabled me to make supplications with firm conviction, persistence and tenacity. So he will accept those supplications.

47

The darkest moment of the night
is the closest to dawn.

(Victor Hugo)

11) WATER FASTING

There was no way I had given up. I increased my supplications and my pleading became more fervent. At the same time, I specialized myself in hair growth.

I searched for new therapeutic methods and did not want to miss any possible solution. Because one thing was clear: The cure was there, I just had to find it!

In parallel with my search, I have been taking certain natural healing products or applying them to my skin.

One day I heard something about water fasting. Namely, that water fasting is supposed to regenerate the immune system. This point alone was enough to motivate me.

Water fasting is a form of therapeutic fasting in which one abstains from all foods, except water, for a certain period of time. It is often performed for health purposes, to cleanse and detoxify the body, to strengthen the immune system and to lose weight.

During water fasting it is important to drink enough water to avoid dehydration. However, it is important to perform water fasting under medical supervision, especially for people with certain health problems or those taking certain medications.

It should also be noted that water fasting is not for everyone and that there are possible risks, such as weakening of the immune system, malnutrition and other health problems.

However, I started to treat myself without medical supervision and precautions. This was dangerous and risky, but I wanted to reach my goal (the cure) as soon as possible and therefore wanted to avoid any detour. At that time, I had only a book on water fasting in my hand as a guide. After that I had acted. But I do not want to give the name of this book, because in retrospect I consider it insufficient and exaggerated.

Anyway, I had decided to do the water fast during the last ten days of Ramadan. So I wanted to kill two birds with one stone. What do I mean by that? The following:

I and many people around me fast during Ramadan anyway. So I would eat nothing from sunrise to sunset anyway. Since I wanted to combine the water fasting with it, so that I do without food completely in the last days and drink only water. Of course, only in the period where the sun has set and until it rises again.

It may sound simple at first (or not), I thought so too. But after that I realized how hard it was: To eat nothing, nothing at all, and drink only water for ten days - and not at any time either, but only after sunset until sunrise. Since in 2018 it was the last ten days of Ramadan the month of June, it was daylight saving time. That means the sun was setting around 9:30pm at the time and rising at about 03:45am. So I only had about six hours to get water.

You, as a reader, might think that I am crazy, but I just wanted to have this done because it might be the cause of curing my disease. My parents wanted to stop it, but I told them I had to do it because of my disease. Although they would have liked it to be different, they couldn't disagree with me.

I have to say that this was a unique, extreme experience for me. It was incredibly hard. I started my water fasting together with a friend in our shared apartment, but after three days he stopped, while I really wanted to last ten days.

To do this, I had taken advantage of my stubbornness, which seems to be a bad trait. Yes, I am a stubborn person. Being stubborn is a bad trait, but we can turn that trait into good things if we want to. For example, if we are stubborn and do not give up on good deeds, we have turned this seemingly bad trait into something good. I wanted to use the power of my stubbornness in this water fasting matter and not give up. And that's what I did.

I didn't want to go to work during those ten days, but just during those ten days, ironically, I was at work more than I normally was. The reason was that due to a lack of teachers, my employer at the time had asked me to substitute. I could refuse. But I didn't. Because I needed the money.

From the third day I was abnormally weakened. And not only weakness and hunger or thirst was the biggest unpredictable problem, but something completely different. The pain. I had never expected that. Since I had no strength left in my body, I had such severe pain in my joints that I could neither lie down nor sit down, let alone stand.

All I wanted to do all the time was sleep, but unfortunately that didn't work either. Before I started this water fast, I thought I would have a lot of free time where I could read a lot of books. That was my idea. But the reality was different: I couldn't read a line of book. Because reading a book requires energy, and I didn't have that energy in the slightest. As I said, even just lying down was difficult for me, let alone reading a book. Impossible.

Most of what I wanted was just to make the time (of water fasting) go by quickly. My favorite thing to do at that time was something I had probably never done before:

I watched videos on YouTube with recipes for dishes on my phone while lying in bed.

The appealing views of delicious dishes soothed me. My stomach was not satiated, but at least this way I satisfied my eyes. And I dreamed of eating these dishes after Lent.

I could never have imagined that I would find myself in such a situation. I could think of nothing else but food.

But metaphysically, this experience was extremely enriching for me. I understood what hunger and thirst really means. In contrast, the normal Ramadan fast seemed like child's play to me (even though you couldn't eat or drink anything for about 18 hours in those summer times). I understood what a great blessing it was to be able to eat and drink anything when one wished. I understood how rich I actually was. Even though I was living in a shared apartment at the time, I had noticed how full our kitchen was with different foods. This experience opened up such an unimaginable dimension with me that I would not have understood with just reading or seeing. To understand it, I would have to experience it.

Nevertheless, I personally would not recommend anyone to try water fasting for ten days - at most for three days and that, under medical supervision. I myself don't plan to do anything like that ever again. There was a time when I fell over backwards on the toilet, but thank God the wall behind me caught me.

On the last day of the fast, I did an enema. An enema refers to the introduction of a liquid into the intestines. I don't want to go into detail, but it is not a simple matter. If you want to try water fasting, you should do an enema at least once, but preferably several times for better results and effective cleansing. Still, I had done it only once and it was very hard for me. But on the last day I really felt how my body and intestines eliminated the toxins. It was a once in a lifetime experience and again I would not recommend it to anyone without a doctor's supervision.

The ten days were over. The eleventh day, when I could slowly become "normal" again, had begun. The book I had used as a guide said that the first ten days after the ten-day water fast were more important than the fast itself. Therefore, the book gave instructions on how and what to eat and drink after the water fast. I followed them. On the eleventh morning I drank a freshly squeezed orange juice, but it was to be two-thirds water. I will never forget that moment. It was as if an energy had been injected into my joints.

Even drinking the freshly squeezed orange juice made me suddenly feel awake and full of energy. Of course, I was also filled with an incredible feeling of happiness. Not only because it tasted so good, but also because of my sense of achievement. I had patiently persevered to the end, and the strength for it had been given to me by the All-Merciful alone.

Now for the result: I had lost a lot of weight. But when I started eating normally again, I was able to eat more than ever before. And the interesting thing is that I just didn't feel full, like the feeling of fullness was gone. I was even a little afraid that I would never feel full again. Of course, that led to a yo-yo effect. I had gained more weight after that than I ever had before. However, after several months, I automatically returned to my previous normal weight.

In relation to my disease alopecia, I had not noticed any direct effect at that time. But because I had detoxified and purified my body, this healing fast could have been one of the reasons for my recovery in the years to come.

12) OXYGEN THERAPY

I had high hopes when I went to an alternative practitioner in Frankfurt for oxygen therapy. After each session I felt very good, but I did not notice any direct positive effect on my skin disease. Since I had to pay a lot of money for it each time due to my financial situation at that time and felt that it did not help to cure my disease, I interrupted the therapy after almost a year.

Nevertheless, I had learned many good tips for a healthy diet and lifestyle from my old but youthful-looking alternative practitioner, for which I am still grateful.

MY ROAD TO RECOVERY

Year 2018. Four years had already passed since my fight against my disease situation had begun. Despite all the failed treatments, my faith in a full recovery coming soon was still very strong. However, there were no signs that could give me hope for recovery. If there was at least a single strand of hair on my body - anywhere, be it my arm, my leg, or anywhere else - I would be incredibly motivated. But no, I haven't had a single hair on my entire body in about four years. Despite this fact, however, I was rock-solidly convinced that I would get all my hair, whiskers, eyebrows and eyelashes back completely. However, I did not know when or how this would happen. But I hoped that it would happen soon.

One Thursday evening, as I was going to my music school in Offenbach for my weekly saz class as usual, I met a new, nice man in our group.[2] The man, who I later learned was named Caner, looked at me kindly as if he knew me from somewhere. Then he told me that his son supposedly had the same disease as me. That's how we got into conversation.

I was very interested in what he had to say. He told me that his fourteen-year-old son was suffering from the same disease as me, and that he had searched far and wide for cures. He had even found the best expert in Turkey, supposedly named "Armless Agor", an Armenian doctor. But even this doctor could not help his son. I don't remember exactly how many years his son had suffered from this disease, but it must have been seven or eight years by then. He went on to tell me that he had finally found a senior physician named Prof. Dr. Schopf at the University Hospital in Mainz. This retired professor had made a name for himself worldwide in his scene and had arranged for his son to get his hair back. Thereupon he showed me

---

[2] Also: The music school is called Medet Aslan - Musikakademie in Offenbach. If you want to learn stringed instrument, you should visit there. My music teacher Medet Aslan is a nice and honorable man with friendly character, who is one of the best Saz stars in Germany; in my opinion even the best.

a few photos of his son, on which he could actually be seen with hair.

After this conversation, I knew that my next stop was the Mainz University Hospital. I researched on the Internet and called the skin outpatient clinic to make an appointment with Mr. Schopf. When they asked me about my insurance, I replied that I had statutory insurance. They then explained that Mr. Schopf only treats private patients and offered me an appointment with another doctor. I finally accepted.

On the agreed date, I went to the University Hospital in Mainz. A young doctor received me and quickly recognized what the problem was. He offered to prescribe the cortisone cream that I had also been prescribed in a previous hospital. I realized that everything was starting all over again. I said I wanted an alternative, but the doctor insisted and said to start with this medication first. Frustrated, I left the clinic.

I talked to my friend Caner about it and told him the story. He told me that his son was also statutory insured, but had still been treated by Mr. Schopf. In addition, his son was treated with DCPC. Mr. Schopf started with a 5% dose and increased it to 12%. My previous doctor at the other clinic had told me that they could do nothing after 2% DCPC. Very interesting.

Well, after I had once again reluctantly applied the prescribed cortisone cream for a month or two, I went to the young doctor at the Mainz University Hospital a second time. He saw that nothing had changed and this time wanted to prescribe a higher dose of cortisone cream. But I didn't want to give in this time. I said that I wanted to be treated with 5% DCPC. He explained that he could not do such a thing. I told him that Mr. Schopf does this very well with his patients. He then responded somewhat gruffly and said that if that was the case, I should go to Mr. Schopf and demand it of him. I replied that they had not accepted me. But he said that with his recommendation I should go to the private outpatient clinic again and make an appointment with Mr. Schopf there.

No sooner said than done. This time I was accepted and could finally make an appointment with Mr. Schopf. Later I learned that if you don't have private insurance, you should say that you are a self-payer. That is the only way to be accepted.

The time had come. I went in to see Mr. Schopf and saw a friendly, calm, older man who radiated his expertise and yet was extremely modest. He was confident and knew exactly what he was doing. I told him my story and he immediately prescribed me a DCPC ointment at a dose of 5%.

After a few months of use, I had seen a few hairs grow on the top of my head. After four or five years, hair finally grew back on my entire body. Although they were minimal, I kept wanting to touch those little spots on my head with my fingers and kept looking in the mirror. My joy was indescribable.

In one of my other appointments with Prof. Schopf, he spoke fleetingly about another drug that could lead to a full recovery, but was very expensive. I told him that I was open to it, but he recommended that I continue to use the conventional drug with a higher dose. Not wanting to disagree with him, the other drug had settled in my mind.

By my next appointment, there was improvement again, but minimal. I then approached him regarding the medication he mentioned the other day and asked if he could prescribe it for me. He said that it was very expensive and that I could buy a car for it.

A car? I wouldn't even care about a house if I suffered from this disease. I asked him how much it would cost. He answered that it would cost about 1,200 € for one month. I told him that I really wanted it because health is the most important thing for me.

When I was so insistent and persistent, he prescribed the medication with a somewhat annoyed and reluctant expression and pressed the prescription into my hand. I walked out and grinned. I knew he wasn't trying to pick my pocket, but I never cared so much about money. The main thing was to get my hair back. I was very happy.

Xeljanz (Tofacitinib)

Xeljanz is a drug containing tofacitinib as the active ingredient and is used to treat rheumatoid arthritis and psoriatic arthritis. It belongs to the group of Janus kinase inhibitors and works by inhibiting certain inflammatory processes in the joints. Xeljanz is available in tablet form and is taken orally. It is important to note that Xeljanz is not suitable for every patient and may not be effective for all types of rheumatoid arthritis or psoriatic arthritis.

So the drug has nothing to do with hair growth. Prof. Schopf said that it came out by chance that this drug also induces a cure for Alopecia Areata.

Quote from Prof. Schopf:

"The efficacy of this drug is documented by at least 50 publications, of which you can check Pubmed[3] on the Internet. The manufacturing company, Pfizer, does not do studies with it because the patent protection is too short to recoup the costs."

After only six months of treatment, I had gotten back more hair than I had ever had since the beginning of my disease (about 4-5 years

---

[3] https://pubmed.ncbi.nlm.nih.gov/?term=xeljanz+alopecia (last call: 10.06.2023)

ago). I was beside myself with joy.

After about a year of treatment, when I went back to Mr. Schopf for an appointment, this sensitive old man looked happier about my improvement than I did.

When I went back to see him after about 2 years, he was so surprised at my improvement or hair growth that he said, "This is a miracle!" At that time, I could not have guessed that this word from my doctor would be the main title of a book that I would one day publish....

I then asked him if he knew of any other cases similar to mine. He said that there were other patients who had successes, but not like mine, because my hair came back completely 100%. Fortunately, after 4-5 years my hair grew back lush and healthy, and it turned out that such a case was not common; so much so that even my experienced doctor witnessed such an incident for the first time.

My beard, eyebrows, eyelashes and also body hair grew back. The order of their growth was as follows: First, my head hair grew. At the same time my beard hair came. After that, with time, body hair grew back. Next to last, after about 2 years, my eyebrows came, but unlike the others, they grew very slowly. And at the very end my eyelashes came. It took about 3-4 years for the eyelashes to come. I was even afraid that the hair roots were destroyed. But thank God, they also grow back again. Now my eyebrows have grown back completely. My beard too. My mustache is back to about 90 % and it continues to grow back. As of June 2023, my eyelashes are about 70% back and continue to grow back. I expect they will also grow back to 100% or more soon.

ABOUT THE MEDICINE

At this significant point in the book, I would like to turn the floor over to my highly esteemed physician, Prof. Dr. Schopf. With extraordinary generosity, he has written down his precious thoughts and observations for this book. It is a truly remarkable preface that I would like to share with all of you at this unique point in the work. It fills me with a deep sense of awe and sincere gratitude that I now have the honor of presenting his words.

Prof. Dr. Schopf is not only an outstanding expert in his field, but also a trusted companion and a true advocate for my story.

In his foreword, Prof. Dr. Schopf reveals not only his deep understanding of the medical world, but also his personal observations that touch the core of my narrative. His astute insights and insightful words have an unparalleled depth and beautifully complement the story I wish to share with you.

It is an extraordinary honor and privilege for me to now share these powerful lines with all of you. The opportunity to present the foreword of my esteemed physician in this book is truly enriching and leaves me humbled.

THE FOREWORD
BY MY DOCTOR
PROF. DR. MED. SCHOPF[4]

---

[4] This foreword has been translated from German to English.

Alopecia areata (AA), i.e. circular hair loss, is one of the most common autoimmune diseases. One in fifty people around the globe may develop it during their lifetime. If you stand in a line of people, you will usually see someone with AA. The disease can appear for the first time as early as preschool age, but also after the age of 70. Mostly it appears in children from the age of 9 or in young adults. There is no gender preference. Hormonal influences are not present in AA. Often psychological triggers are searched for, for which, however, no evidence is found in larger examinations. However, it cannot be excluded that severe psychological injuries or bereavement may precede AA in predisposed individuals. The disease usually shows one or more circular bald patches on the hairy head, but other areas such as the beard area in men or the rest of the body hair can also be affected. In the worst case, the disease progresses into total or universal hair loss, i.e. AA totalis or AA universalis. The disease usually starts suddenly within about 3 weeks. Many patients experience itching or even pain of the scalp. Tufts of hair falling out may be present, in which case AA totalis will usually follow.

So-called exclamation mark hairs characterize the clinical picture, i.e. the hairs show thinning at the scalp, then they become thicker and break off after about 3-5 mm in length. In the case of total hair loss, flat horny pads can be found in the hair root exits when magnifying with a magnifying glass, which indicate degenerated hair. Black dots can also be seen as residual hair in the scalp. Affected individuals especially suffer from loss of eyebrows and eyelashes, such as wind or sun exposure. In addition, one finds rough nails, dimpled nails (trachyonychia, onychosis punctata) or increased red lunulae.

Interestingly, AA can occur in all animals with fur, in certain laboratory mice or rats, which is used experimentally, also in dogs, bears or horses. About 40% of patients with AA also present with Hashimoto's thyroiditis, which is an autoimmune disease of the thyroid gland. AA also frequently occurs in patients with a tendency to neurodermatitis.

Hair growth shapes the image of a person. The loss of hair leads to strong psychological discomfort and shame, so that quite a few patients with AA have to visit psychologists or psychiatrists. Practically all patients with AA suffer from their appearance, especially if they are no longer recognized in their home town with AA totalis. For most patients, AA is a psychological disaster.

It is now known that hyperfunction of the immune system leads to hair loss. Hair possesses an immunological privilege in the form that hair roots are not attacked by the immune system. When this privilege is lost for unclear reasons, cytotoxic CD8-positive T-lymphocytes attack the hair roots like a swarm of bees, leading to hair loss in the form of exclamation mark hairs. Fortunately, the immunological attack spares the stem cells located above the hair roots, allowing hair to grow back even after years of loss. Within a year, the chance of spontaneous healing is greatest, but by no means reliable. AA shows an unpredictable course.

There are several options for treatment. The first step is often a corticosteroid cream, which is almost never sufficient. Systemic therapy with corticosteroids succeeds in making the hair grow, but a higher dose is needed for this, which causes many side effects such as full moon face. After reducing the dose or stopping the therapy, the hair falls out again.

For about 50 years it has been known that creating an allergic contact eczema on the scalp creates an environment that hair can grow again. Diphenyl cyclopropenone or quadratic acid dibutyl ester dissolved in acetone is used for this purpose. Furthermore, by applying dithranol, a local immunosuppressant for psoriasis, it is possible to get hair growth after about 6 months, which can be shown in the half-side experiment. These are irritants, which make it difficult to apply, so that reputable dermatologists refrain from such therapy.

Unexpectedly, in a 2015 psoriasis treatment study, it was found that a newly developed immunosuppressant class of compounds, the Janus kinase (JAK) inhibitors /citinibe, i.e., tofacitinib could additionally cause hair to grow in a patient with AA. The patient had no hair for 14 years and then got a lion's mane. This is considered a milestone in the discovery of AA. Janus kinases transmit inflammatory signals from the cell surface to the nucleus, which controls the production of inflammatory mediators. JAK inhibitors such as tofacitinib, baricitinib, upadacitinib and others succeed in producing hair growth in AA. The therapy must be taken for many months, can lead to side effects and is very expensive. The therapy costs amount to approximately from 1,000 € per month. Health insurance companies and insurers usually refuse to cover the cost, even though baricitinib is approved as a drug for AA. For the other Citinibe, treatment is "off-label", i.e. there is no approval for it, and the risk is borne by the physician. Hair growth in AA is considered a lifestyle measure by payers. Of course, this is not true at all, rather it is about the treatment of the autoimmune disease AA.

This book vividly presents a realistic picture of AA. Through our therapy with Tofacitinib the author got his hair back. We wish the book a good spreading. Affected patients can learn from it and take courage that their hair will grow again.

Prof. Dr. med. Rudolf Schopf

Department of Dermatology, University Medical Center Mainz

June 2023

MY TRANSFORMATION IN PICTURES

In this section, I will share with you the photos that my doctor took during the exams to give you a concrete impression of my change.

Date: 18.07.2018

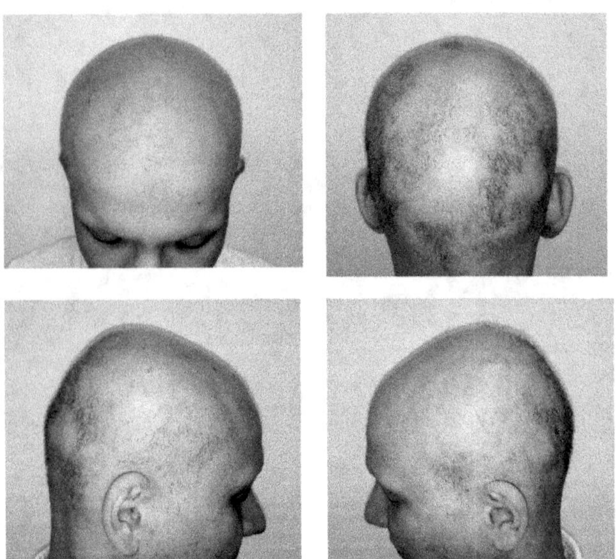

Date: 15.08.2018

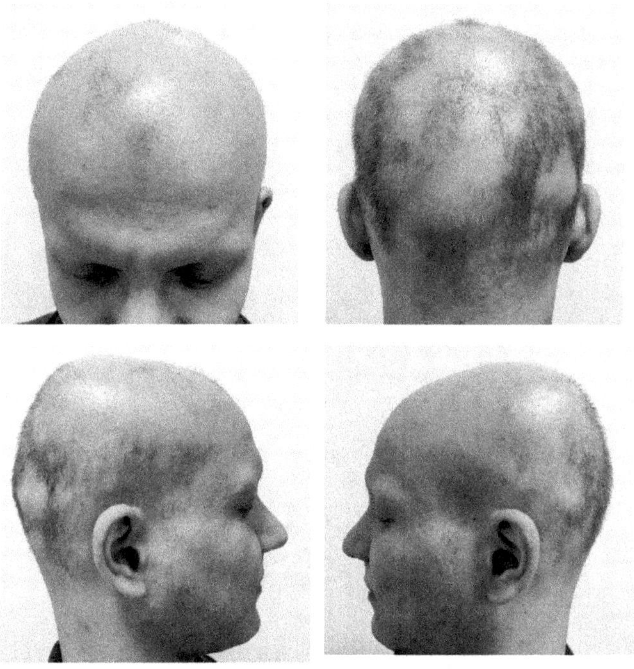

Date: 19.09.2018

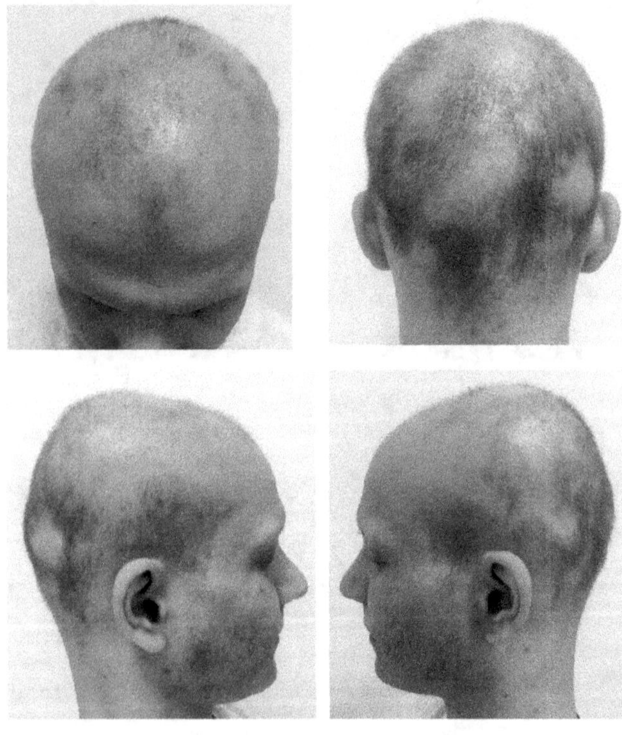

Date: 12.12.2018

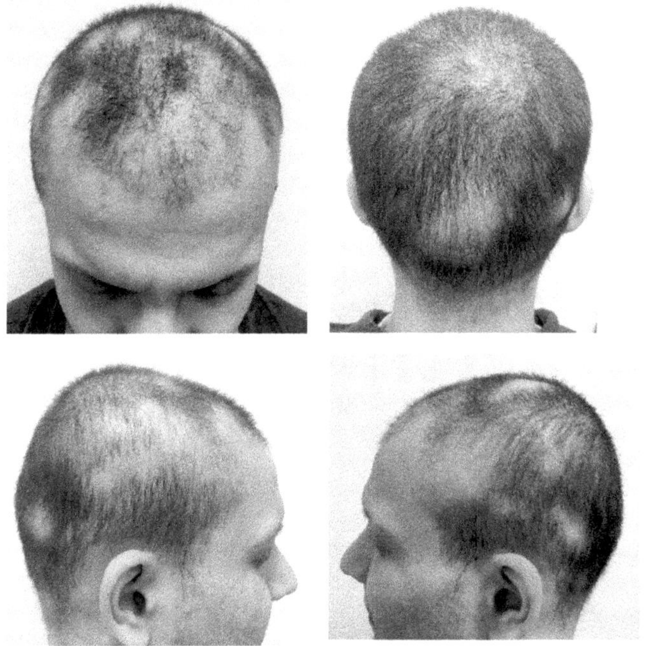

Date: 22.01.2019

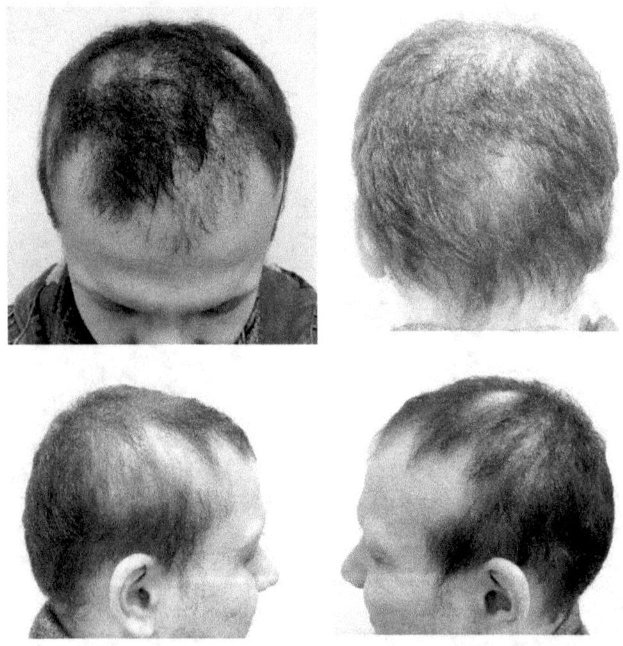

Date: 26.02.2019

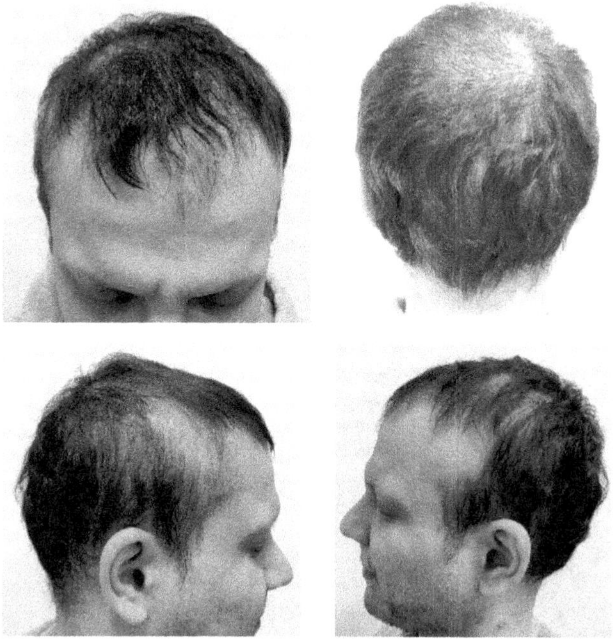

Date: 14.05.2019

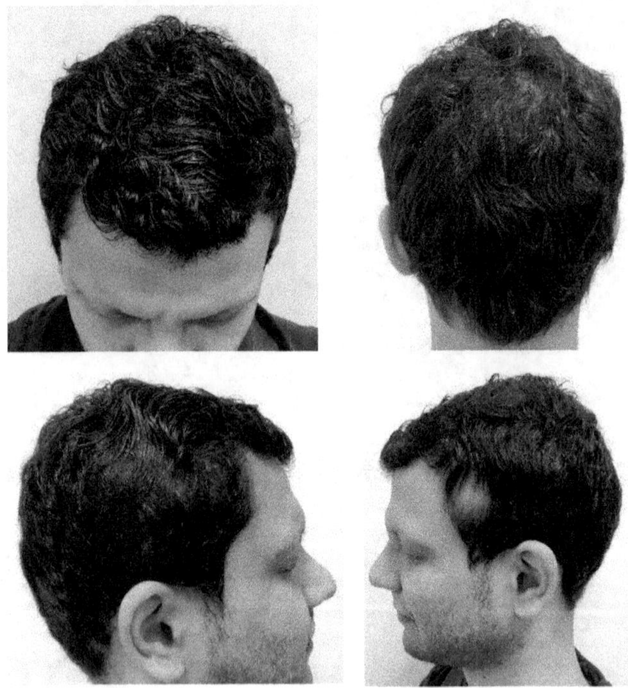

Date: 09.07.2019

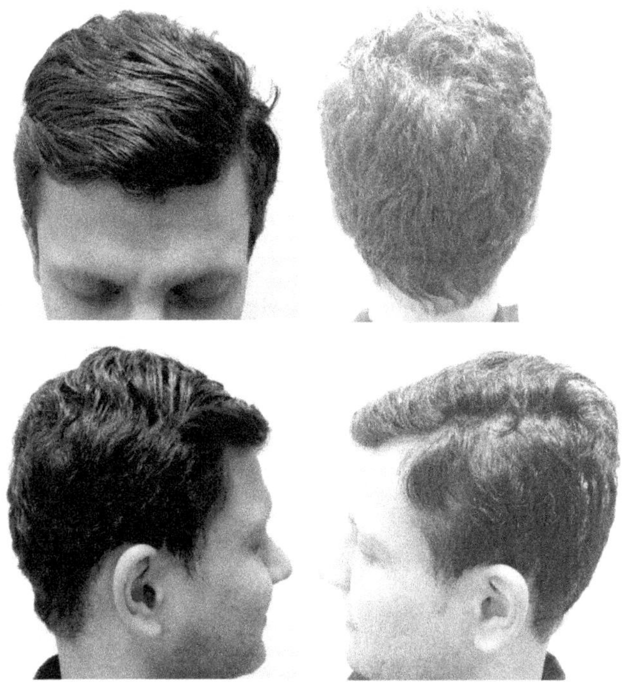

Date: 02.09.2020

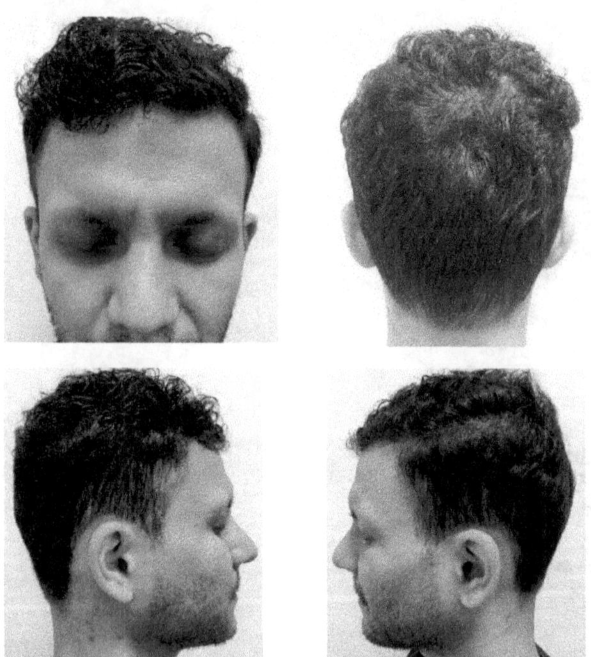

"THIS IS A MIRACLE" SAID MY DOCTOR
REVERSING HAIR LOSS AND ALOPECIA

Date: 25.11.2020

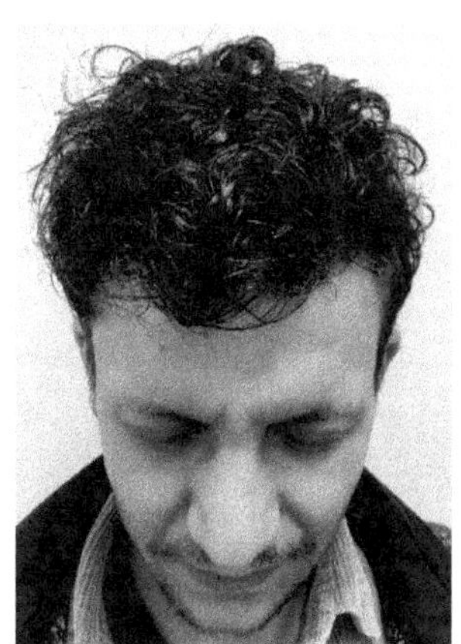

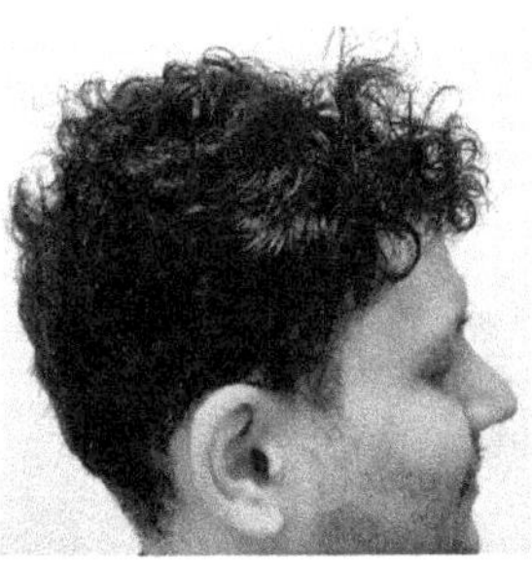

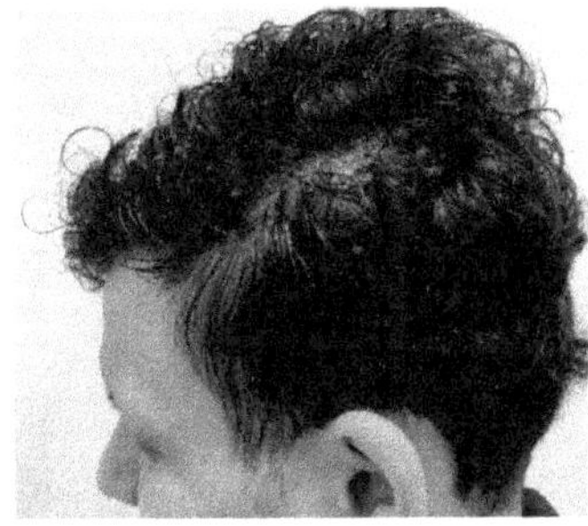

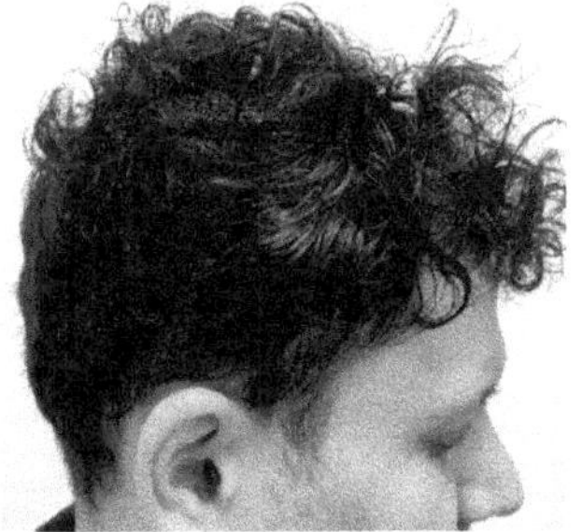

Date: 09.02.2022

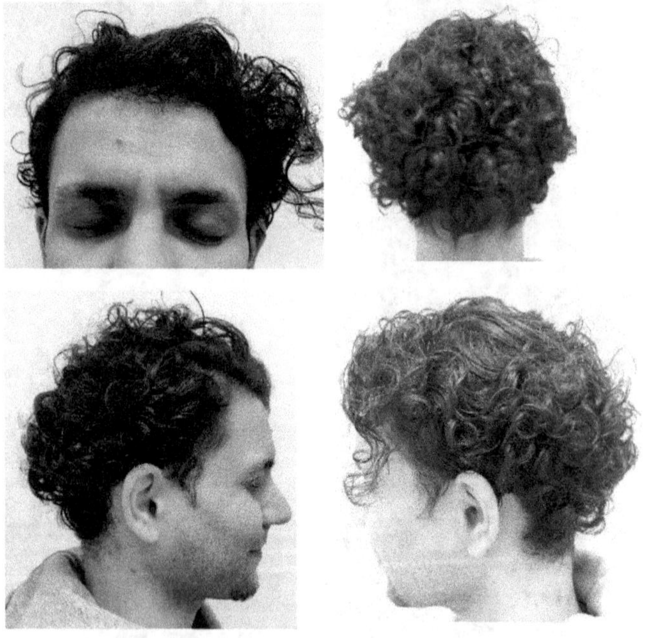

"THIS IS A MIRACLE" SAID MY DOCTOR
REVERSING HAIR LOSS AND ALOPECIA

After four years of treatment, I look like this (September 2022):

(Photo was taken by myself)

Some questions about the medicine

Before I answer some questions about Xeljanz (tofacitinib), I would like to emphasize that you should definitely take this drug under the prescription and supervision of a physician.

The effect of Xeljanz may naturally vary from person to person. Unfortunately, there is no guarantee that the drug will work for everyone. Here is a section from PubMed:

Objective: We sought to evaluate the safety and efficacy of the Janus kinase 1/3 inhibitor, tofacitinib, in a series of patients over an extended period of time.

Methods: This is a retrospective study of patients age 18 years or older with AA with at least 40% scalp hair loss treated with tofacitinib. The primary end point was the percent change in Severity of Alopecia Tool (SALT) score during treatment.

Results: Ninety patients met inclusion criteria. Of 65 potential responders to therapy, defined as those with alopecia totalis or alopecia universalis with duration of current episode of disease of 10 years or less or alopecia areata, 77% achieved a clinical response, with 58% of patients achieving greater than 50% change in SALT score over 4 to 18 months of treatment. Patients with AA experienced a higher percent change in SALT score than did patients with alopecia totalis or alopecia universalis (81.9% vs 59.0%). Tofacitinib was well tolerated, and there were no serious adverse events.[5]

Does the medicine have side effects?

---

[5] https://pubmed.ncbi.nlm.nih.gov/27816293/ (last call: 10.06.2023)

This medicine can have many side effects. Here I would like to emphasize the word "can", because not all patients experience side effects. For example, I did not experience any side effects even though I had my blood checked every six months. My doctor had reassured me and said that if there were no side effects in six to twelve months, it was an indication that I was tolerating the drug well and that there would be no side effects in the future.

I took the risk myself and accepted the possible side effects, but of course everyone should decide for themselves. The dose in which the drug is taken is also important. I personally took it twice a day at a dose of 5 mg. Detailed information on possible side effects can be found on the Internet or in the package insert.

Does the medicine have any disadvantages?

The biggest disadvantage of this drug is clearly its price. Unfortunately, it is very expensive. In 2019, the price of 56 film-coated tablets with the dose of 5 mg was about 1,280 €. The price has gradually decreased a bit. In 2023, the price is about €939. If you take it twice a day, it will be used up within a month.

Normally, health insurance companies do not cover the costs if you have statutory insurance. If you have private insurance, they usually do. Since I am voluntarily insured, my health insurance did not cover the costs. That is why I asked Prof. Schopf for an expert opinion. The good man approved it. I sent it to my health insurance and asked them to cover the costs, but they refused.

Here is that expert opinion:

JGU UNIVERSITÄTSmedizin.
MAINZ

Hautklinik und Poliklinik

Direktor: Univ.-Prof. Dr. med. Stephan Grabbe

Prof. Dr. Rudolf Schopf
Privatambulanz
Geb. 401, EG
Langenbeckstr. 1
55131 Mainz
Telefon +49 (0) 6131 17-7112
Telefax +49 (0) 6131 17-3470
http://www.hautklinik-mainz.de

Mainz, 18. Juli 2018

Gutachten zur Vorlage bei der BMW-BKK

Patient   **Herr Selim Dursun *06.04.1990**

Sehr geehrte Damen und Herren,

wir berichten über o.g. Pat., der seit 4 Jahren an Alopecia areata totalis leidet.
Die bisherigen Behandlungsversuche mit Lokaltherapeutika waren erfolglos, wovon man sich
Leicht überzeugen kann.
In der Zwischenzeit liegen mehrere positive Heilungs-Berichte von Serien von Pat. vor, die mit Xeljanz®
(Tofacitinib) 2 x 5 mg/d behandelt werden (vgl. reichlich Literatur bei Pubmed). Xeljanz ist für die
Behandlung der rheumatoiden Arthritis und Psoriasis-Arthritis zugelassen.
Wir bitten daher die ▮▮▮▮▮▮ die Kosten dafür für zunächst 6 Monate zu übernehmen.
Bei Fragen stehen wir gerne zur Verfügung.

Mit freundlichen Grüßen

Prof. Dr. Rudolf Schopf, FAAD
Oberarzt

But I didn't give up and sued my health insurance company. I was in court. Once again I asked my hero Prof. Schopf for an expert opinion, once again he helped me.

Here is the expert opinion for the court:

Direktor: Univ.-Prof. Dr. med. Stephan Grabbe

Prof. Dr. Rudolf Schopf
Privatsprechstunde
Geb. 401 EG
Langenbeckstr. 1
55131 Mainz
Telefon +49 (0) 6131 17-7112
Telefax +49 (0) 6131 17-3470
http://www.hautklinik-mainz.de

Mainz, 5. November 2019

Gutachten zur Vorlage bei der Krankenversicherung / beim Gericht

Patient   **Herr Selim Dursun *06.04.1990**

Sehr geehrte Damen und Herren,

Wir berichten über o.g. Pat., der sich in unserer regelmäßigen ambulanten Behandlung befindet wegen der Diagnose:

Alopecia areata

Bei der ersten Vorstellung hier vor ca. 1 Jahr wies der Pat. praktisch keine Haare im Bereich des Kopfes auf, auch die Körperhaare waren größtenteils ausgefallen. Die zuerst begonnene Therapie mit Diphenyl-Cyclopropenon zur Erzeugung eines allergischen Kontaktekzems hierbei fruchtete nicht.

Daraufhin haben wir off-label eine Behandlung mit Xeljanz ® (Tofacitinib) 2 x 5 mg begonnen wobei es zusehends zu neuen Haaren bis hin zu einem vollem Haarwuchs mit Locken gekommen ist. Aufgrund des hohen Preises haben wir die dann Dosis auf nur 1x5 mg/Tag reduziert, worunter ein vermehrtes Ausfallen der Haare nicht zu übersehen ist. Dies zeigt, dass eine Dosis von 2 x 5 mg eingenommen werden sollte.

Leider ist Xeljanz sehr teuer (56 Tbl. 1087,55 Euro). Darüber hinaus bestehen keine Doppelblindstudien dazu. Andererseits ist die Wirksamkeit anhand von mindestens 50 Publikationen dokumentiert, wovon man sich bei Pubmed im Internet vergewissern kann. Die Herstellerfirma Pfizer macht damit keine Studien, weil der Patentschutz zu kurz ist, um die Kosten wieder hereinzubekommen.

Alopecia areata ist keine lebensgefährliche Erkrankung; dennoch leiden die Pat. in hohem Ausmaß darunter. Nicht wenige Pat. benötigen deswegen Psychotherapie. Das Erscheinungsbild ändert sich in großem Maße, die Pat. berichten, dass sie z.B. von ihrer Umfeld nicht mehr erkannt werden. Dem gegenüber steht jetzt die relativ einfache Behandlung mit Xeljanz, deren Problem der hohe Preis ist, den man verständlicherweise umgehen will.

Wir bitten daher den Kostenträger die Kosten für dieses Medikament zumindest für die nächsten sechs Monate zu übernehmen. Bei Fragen stehen wir gerne zur Verfügung.

Mit freundlichen Grüßen

Prof. Dr. Rudolf Schopf, FAAD
Oberarzt der Klinik

To my recollection, the court proceedings lasted about 1-1.5 years. Unfortunately, I lost in the end because my health insurance company argued that this was a cosmetic problem and not a medical problem. The court had ruled in favor of the health insurance company, which I found ridiculous.

However, I still needed to take the tablets and finally found a way to get them from abroad at a much cheaper price. I realized that the prices of medicines vary from country to country, so I started to buy medicines from another country.

Why did it work so well for me ?

The real, true reason why it worked so well for me is quite clear: The Lord of all things has willed it so. He wanted to give me back the hair he had taken from me. I am very grateful to Him for that.

However, if you were to ask me what causes might be responsible for this decision, I would say this: I did my best to manage the causes of my illness and do everything in my power for a cure. I think it is a requirement of respect for the system established by the Creator.

What have I done?

1- I have not only made fervent supplications myself, but also asked other people for their supplications. Especially through donations for orphans in Africa, I have received many supplications from orphans.
2- I never gave up hope and I was one hundred percent sure that I would be cured very soon.
3- I never stopped fighting. Again and again I tried more therapies, sometimes even several at the same time.
4- I have always educated myself and increased my knowledge about my disease, hair growth, nutrition and healthy living.
5- In addition to my treatment with Xeljanz (Tofacitinib), I have also used many other supplements that I consider essential. Supplements are a big topic and I will explain them in detail in the last chapter of the book.

Our role in the fight against diseases is to continue to do our best to manage the causes; always patient, without giving up, without despairing.

Our greatest weakness lies in giving up. The most certain way to succeed is always to try just one more time.
(Thomas Edison)

What if I were not healed?

It is actually impossible for me to answer this question because I am not in that situation. I really don't know, but I would wish it had I not been healed:

... I would continue to make fervent supplications and never give up my hope.

... I would have tried to convince my heart that it is better for me to be sick than to be well. Because the Infinite Mercy that sent us into the world wants only the best for us. But I would still ask Him for health. On the whole, I think I would continue to follow the five points from the previous part.

In addition, I would perhaps try a meat diet. There are reports of people with chronic diseases being cured by this diet.

> The meat diet, also known as the carnivore diet, is a very restricted diet that eats mainly meat and animal products such as eggs and dairy. Vegetables, fruits and other plant foods are usually avoided. The idea behind this is that meat and animal products contain all the nutrients the body needs to stay healthy, while plant foods may be unnecessary or even harmful. However, it is important to note that most nutritionists and health experts do not recommend this type of diet because it is not balanced and lacks many important nutrients that are necessary for health. It can lead to deficiencies and health problems if followed for a long period of time. A doctor should always be consulted before following such a diet.

I call myself a flexitarian, but might have done this diet exceptionally for recovery.

THE MYSTERY

Just as it is no coincidence that not even a leaf falls from a tree by chance, my encounter with this disease was no coincidence. I knew that my Lord gave me this disease and that He wants only the best for me. And I also knew that there was a great wisdom behind my illness, but of which I was not aware.

But despite all this, I was very sad because of my illness. It caused me inner pain, also because it hit me when I was 24 years old, in the middle of my youth. Over the years, my pain related to the disease increased instead of me getting used to it. Because during the most precious years of my life, I had to deal with complete hair loss and it hurt me a lot. Again and again I thought that those years would never come back.

However, something quite interesting has happened. I am now 33 years old and when I ask people how old they think I am, they answer that I look 24 years old at the most. If I cut my beard, I look even younger.

If you remember, I was 24-25 years old when I lost my hair.

Do you think that might be a coincidence?

THE LAST CHAPTER:

YOUR HEALING STORY

NATURAL AND DURABLE HAIR GROWTH FORMULA

Now we come to a great headline: The natural and consistent hair growth formula.[6]

As in the previous chapters of this book, I will try to share with you all my secrets, all my knowledge and all my valuable experiences on this subject in an open and authentic way. From here, hopefully, your healing story begins.

What is the likelihood of genetic hair loss?

If you go to a dermatologist for hair loss and ask for help, there is a very good chance that your doctor will tell you that your hair loss is genetic. As a result, he will most likely prescribe you some kind of chemicals to slow down or postpone the hair loss process. Unfortunately, I don't recall ever hearing any other scenario on this.

Is the problem really only in our genetics? No! According to Dr. Peter Jentschura and Josef Lohkämper, 85% of hair loss is caused by the loss of minerals in the scalp. The body extracts these minerals to neutralize hyperacidity in the body. Only 1% of hair loss is genetic, while another 1% is due to hormonal changes. Medications, preservatives, pesticides, environmental and residential toxins, and amalgam in the teeth contribute 5% to hair loss, according to them, while stress and negative emotions are responsible for 3%.

The remaining 5% of hair loss is caused by mineral losses during pregnancy. This is because after pregnancy, the body's mineral depots are often depleted, which can also lead to hair loss. To stop this hair loss, they recommend replenishing minerals and avoiding acidity in the body.[6]

---

[6] Dr.h.c. Peter Jentschura - Josef Lohkämper "Health through purification" May 2010.

If the hair roots are not completely destroyed, the hair can of course grow back. However, this may take a little longer. The body, as long as it is not overacidified and has sufficient resources, can produce new hair. In this case, one should have patience.

So according to Dr. Peter Jentschura and Josef Lohkämper, only 1% of hair loss is due to genetic factors. This means that the probability of hair falling out due to genetic factors is very low. However, it is important to note that everyone is different and there are several factors that can influence hair loss, including hormones, environmental factors, stress and other health problems.

Which doctors should we see?

It is important to consult a really competent doctor in order to determine the exact causes of hair loss and to get a suitable treatment for it. For this purpose, I would not save from costs and in any case look for a competent private doctor. Unfortunately, many of the doctors who treat patients with statutory health insurance are bound by certain regulations or contracts. Therefore, most of them are not always completely open and always prescribe the same drugs, because they have certain contractual bindings. But private doctors are usually more open and freer in this respect.

It is also no coincidence that many doctors do not talk about simple home remedies, vitamins, minerals and natural supplements, as well as detoxification and deacidification of the body, when in fact they could solve our problems quite easily and consistently. Instead, they try to sell us certain chemicals that cause our bodies and hair to become addicted. Some of these chemicals cause us to become addicted and as soon as we stop taking them, we fall back into the initial situation. To avoid this, we have to pay huge amounts of money all the time. The pharmaceutical companies are the main beneficiaries of this. To make it clear that I am not spreading conspiracy theories here, I recommend the book "Deadly Medicine and Organized Crime: How the Pharmaceutical Industry Corrupts Healthcare" by Peter C. Gøtzsche.

https://hawloo.eu/links/en-gotzsche

The scientificity of our mentioned treatment methods

Some might say that there are insufficient clinical, scientifically valid studies on these natural hair growth formulas mentioned in the book. Even if that were true, would it really make sense to label these methods as false or worthless just for that reason?

I myself am an academic (M.A.) who completed his master's degree in Germany, and I naturally place a lot of value on scientific studies. Nevertheless, I believe that one should never rely exclusively on scientific studies. Here are some reasons why:

1- It is well known that some pharmaceutical companies deliberately avoid double-blind studies of some drugs because it is not worthwhile for them in terms of costs, since the patent protection is too short. For example, this is the case with my drug Xeljanz (tofacitinib), as Prof. Schopf also clearly mentioned in his expert opinion (see chapter: Disadvantages of Xeljanz). So would it make sense to claim that this drug is useless just because there are no double-blind studies with 100,000 subjects? Moreover, we should not forget that according to Prof. Schopf there are more than 50 scientific articles on this drug on PubMed.

2- Donald Light, a sociologist and professor of comparative health policy at the Medical and Dental University of New Jersey, has found in his study that many drugs that are considered to be scientifically and medically validated do not, in fact, work. He even goes so far as to claim that their effectiveness has never been proven. Furthermore, he states that, unfortunately, there is a great deal of fraud in the approval of many drugs.[7]

Hereby I am not trying to doubt the trust in all medications, but I just want to point out that one should not necessarily limit oneself only to medically approved medications. Because even with these drugs you can not rely 100% on their reliability.

3- Unfortunately, there are enough cases where studies have been bought or falsified. Unfortunately, the pharmaceutical industry is often more concerned with money than with the well-being of patients. For this reason, the effectiveness of some dietary supplements is also constantly questioned or even denigrated.[8] This is because dietary supplements do not have to be prescribed by doctors and can be sold by any (small) company on the market.

4- To believe in the efficacy of some treatments and natural medicines, a scientific study is not necessarily required. This is because there is no rule that says that a remedy without

---

[7] https://www.zentrum-der-gesundheit.de/bibliothek/medikamente/nebenwirkungen-medikamente/studien-pharmaindustrie (last call: 10.06.2023)

[8] https://www.zentrum-der-gesundheit.de/bibliothek/sonstige-informationen/medizin-und-forschung/wissenschaftliche-studien-medizin-ia (last call: 10.06.2023)

an acceptable scientific study is necessarily wrong or not reliable. There are many herbs and natural home remedies that have worked successfully for centuries and are confirmed by many people. To me, that is sufficient conviction for their effectiveness, even if there is no study for them. Many people do not always question the background of a study, which an American journalist proved by sending a completely falsified study to 300 journals and was accepted by 157 journals without review.[9]

It may be that these cases are only isolated incidents, and I would like to believe in that. However, I would like to express herewith that one should not rely too much on so-called "scientific studies" and limit oneself exclusively to them, while rejecting proven remedies that have not been scientifically tested.

However, this does not mean that the natural hair growth formulas and methods I mention in this book are unscientific. There are enough studies on many of the approaches listed in this book that I will mention or link in a footnote if possible, as far as they are known to me.

Of course, this book is not a scientific medical book. However, this fact does not make the value of the information in this book therefore low. Only my own personal experience with these natural methods could convince me of their effectiveness. I myself look about ten years younger and have full and strong hair, while many of my peers or younger people look ten years older and unfortunately have long since lost their hair.

---

[9] https://www.zentrum-der-gesundheit.de/bibliothek/sonstige-informationen/medizin-und-forschung/wissenschaftliche-studien-faelschung-ia (last call: 10.06.2023)

Is (genetic) baldness reversible?

If baldness is caused by something like radiation, normally the hair should come back no matter what. But whether a "genetically caused" bald spot or partial bald spot can come back depends on a case-by-case basis. Why I write "genetically caused" in quotes is because the background for a "genetically caused" hair loss is actually not always genetics, but the reasons described below here in the book. Because as mentioned before, genetic hair loss is estimated at 1%, with the 99% being due to other reasons. But the mistakes made can be a trigger for the 1%.

The good news is that hair follicles can shrink with prolonged rest, but they don't always die right away, so sometimes they can be reactivated. If you look closely at balding, you'll see that most people have very small, thin hairs, but they don't continue to grow. This shows that the hair follicles surrounding the hair root are still present and can eventually be reactivated. Activation of hair follicles occurs when they are supplied with sufficient nutrients from the hair base. However, if they are not supplied with sufficient nutrients, this may be due to the hereditary hypersensitivity of the hair follicles to the hormone DHT (dihydrotestosterone) and thus (partial) baldness may form.

One might assume that by providing the hair base with sufficient nutrients, baldness could be eliminated. However, unfortunately, the matter is not so simple. Often the nutrients do not reach the hair floor. The hair floor has fine hair follicles in which the hair root is attached. There are even finer blood vessels located to supply the hair follicles. And it is these fine vessels and the tissue around the hair follicles that are often places where waste products or waste products accumulate.

Slags are parts of harmful substances that we take in with our food, but mostly they are waste products that our body produces itself and should normally get rid of (via kidneys or intestines). Slags also include neutralized acids, which is why we also speak of hyperacidity.

When there are too many slags or when the organs that are supposed to get rid of them are overloaded, our body first stores them - preferably where they can do the least harm, e.g. in the hair floor, with the motto: "Better a bald head than sick organs." But when slags are deposited in the scalp, they clog the fine blood vessels that should supply the scalp and hair roots with nutrients. The fine lymphatic vessels that should remove waste from the hair floor are also clogged. So now the hair follicles and hair roots are surrounded by waste products, which they can no longer get rid of due to clogged drainage paths. At the same time, nutrients can no longer get through, at least not in the required quantity. The result: hair loss.

It may all sound a little complicated at first, but if you are affected by hair loss, the rest of this book can be invaluable to you. So keep at it, and you'll find that the logic behind it isn't actually that hard. Once you understand the logic, all that's left is the practical application, and that's entirely in your hands. Let's get started!

Everything is going to be fine in the end.
If it's not fine it's not the end.

(Oscar Wilde)

INTRODUCTION TO NATURAL HAIR GROWTH FORMULA

The holistic form of therapy for hair loss consists of deacidification and remineralization of the body, as a healthy physiology of hair is based on these mechanisms. A study conducted by the Center of Health in 2007 shows that this form of therapy allowed 100% of participants to stop their hair loss and 90% even achieved new hair growth.[10]

This alternative approach to the natural treatment of hair loss, unlike the traditional medical method, is a holistic therapy that benefits not only the hair, but the entire body. The main focus of this therapy is **deacidification**, **detoxification** and **remineralization**, which apply to all types of hair loss, as naturopathic medicine considers the demineralization of the hair floor as the main reason.

However, a simple solution, such as taking mineral tablets, is not enough. It is important to load the body with as few acids as possible, neutralize the existing acids and remove the slags from the body to remineralize it. If one does not do this, the slags can accumulate in the body and lead to further health problems, including hair loss.[11]

---

[10] p. 18, https://www.yumpu.com/de/document/read/71180677/haarausfall-studie-joico-onlineshop-vicopura (last call: 10.06.2023)

[11] http://www.haarausfall-therapie.net/natuerliche-haarausfallbehandlung.html (last call: 10.06.2023)

Now we come to the practical and technical part. In the following, I would like to take up the three focal points of the natural hair growth formula one after the other:

1) Deacidification

2) Purification

3) Remineralization

In the next section, I will give a summary of my natural treatment program (4).

I will then explain how hair growth can be promoted externally and what factors should be considered (5).

Finally, I will present other important natural healing methods (6) for hair growth.

Well, let's get started!

1) DEACIDIFICATION

There are enough confirming studies in science about hyperacidity and deacidification. In the footnote area you will find some links to these studies.[12]

How does the hyperacidity in our body arise?

Our modern lifestyle and unhealthy eating habits can cause our bodies to become over-acidic. Acidosis refers to a condition where our blood has a pH that is too low, making it more acidic. This can lead to various health problems.

There are many factors that can contribute to hyperacidity. These include excessive consumption of acid-forming foods such as meat, cheese and dairy products, and too little alkaline-rich or neutral foods such as vegetables and fruits. Stress, both acute and chronic, can also lead to acidosis. When we are under stress, hormonal changes can occur in the body that affects our acid-base balance.

Environmental stresses such as air pollution and pesticides can also contribute to hyperacidity. However, the body has natural mechanisms to regulate pH and restore the acid-base balance. For example, the kidneys and lungs can help eliminate excess acids.

However, when the body is overloaded, the acid-base balance can be disturbed. When there are too many acids in the body, the body's natural neutralization mechanisms can no longer be sufficient to restore the balance. This can lead to symptoms such as fatigue,

---

[12] https://pubmed.ncbi.nlm.nih.gov/17658124/ (last call: 10.06.2023)
https://journals.lww.com/jasn/pages/articleviewer.aspx?year=2006&issue=11000&article=00036&type=Fulltext (last call: 10.06.2023)
https://pubmed.ncbi.nlm.nih.gov/21481501/ (last call: 10.06.2023)

headaches and digestive problems, and in the long term increase the risk of various diseases.

Although we cannot control every factor, we have a great influence on the most important factor, which is our diet.

To regulate acid-alkaline balance through diet, it is important to be aware of the foods that are acidic and alkaline.

There are some known factors that can contribute to hyperacidity of the body, including coffee, black tea, phosphoric acid (e.g. in cola), nicotine, fruit acid, sugary drinks, alcohol (especially high-proof), meat, fat and sugar. But negative emotions, stress, noise, smog, lack of exercise and sports can also contribute to hyperacidity.

Fruits and vegetables are usually considered alkaline, although there are also some fruits that are rather acidic. However, there is often disagreement on this point. More importantly, all foods that grow in nature are healthier than convenience foods that are high in sugar and fat or meat. By eating vegetables and fruits, you can make sure to get enough alkaline nutrients. For example, potatoes and carrots are a good source of natural alkaline.

However, it should be noted that pesticides on fruits and vegetables can also be acidic. To avoid these effects, fruits and vegetables can be cleaned with a sodium hydroxide solution or treated with hydrogen peroxide to draw out the pesticides.

Alcohol is matabolized in acids in the body. Due to its dehydrating effect, it removes water and important minerals from the body. This is particularly the case with high-proof alcohol. Ideally, alcohol should be completely avoided during deacidification or at least reduced as much as possible to help the body return to a healthy state more quickly.

Smoking is also not healthy, as it damages the lungs and impairs the body's ability to detoxify. The cilia in the lungs, which are responsible for cleansing, are destroyed and the lungs cannot detoxify as quickly as would be optimal. The lungs are also responsible for exhaling acidic carbon dioxide. Logically, the better this works, the healthier you become.

Consequences and symptoms of hyperacidity

Over-acidification of the body can lead to a variety of negative consequences, including sleep disorders, weight problems, skin problems, difficulty concentrating, sweating and frequent sickness. In addition, hyperacidity can also lead to hair loss, fatigue, menstrual cramps, cellulite, headaches, fatigue, depression, inflammation, eczema and allergies.

An unbalanced acid-alkaline ratio can cause a variety of symptoms. If you notice several of the following ailments, you should consider over-acidification of your body: Headaches, migraines, allergies, heartburn, digestive problems, insomnia, gingivitis, obesity, underweight, skin blemishes, diabetes, menstrual cramps, cellulite, concentration problems, infections, inflammation, muscle cramps, joint pain, high blood pressure and hair loss.

In some cases, hyperacidity can also be a major factor in diseases such as heart attack, cancer, diabetes, gout, osteoporosis, rheumatism and asthma, as these diseases can only survive in an acidic environment.

Determination of the pH value of the body

Are you unsure whether your body is acidic? Then a pH indicator test strip will give you a reliable answer. This test measures the pH value of your organism and informs you whether your body is balanced, alkaline or acidic. A value between 1 and 7 on the scale of the test strip indicates hyperacidity, from a value of 7 a balanced acid-base balance prevails, between 8 and 14 the bases predominate in the body.

The optimal pH value for our blood is in the range 7.35 to 7.45. However, this is a very narrow range that is almost impossible to achieve. A value between 7 and 8 is ideal. However, it must be taken into account that the value fluctuates during the day and depends on the time of day and the last meal eaten.

To test your acid-base balance, you'll need a pH indicator test strip, which you can buy at a pharmacy. You can also test it yourself at home by simply ordering it online here:

https://hawloo.eu/links/ph

There are several methods for testing:

1. Method:

Take a measurement three days in a row at different times (morning, noon, evening). You can either urinate directly onto the test strip or collect your urine in a container. Write down the results. Then calculate the average value of all 9 values, and you will get a pretty meaningful evaluation of your acid-base balance.

2. Method:

For a more accurate result, it is recommended to perform the urine test five times a day. Before breakfast, i.e. on an empty stomach, the pH value should be between 5 and 6.5, which is considered slightly acidic.

- 1-2 hours after breakfast, the result should be alkaline or slightly acidic, with a value of 6.5 to 8.
- 1-2 hours after lunch, the pH should be alkaline and preferably between 8 and 8.5.
- 1-2 hours after dinner, the pH should also be basic, with a value of 8 to 8.5.

3. Method:

If the 1st and 2nd methods were too elaborate for you, you can use this 3rd method.

Here you can perform the test twice a day, 1-2 hours after lunch and 1-2 hours after dinner. In both cases the result should be alkaline.

Why is the acid-base balance important?

Acids include, for example, stomach acid, fatty acid and amino acid, while bases include magnesium, sodium and calcium. Bases are the counterpart to acids and help neutralize and remove them.

Our body works ceaselessly to balance the ratio of acid to base by neutralizing excess acids through its buffering systems - blood, lymph, lungs, tissues, intestines and kidneys. This process is critical to maintaining a healthy blood PH level and prevents dangerous buildup in the tissues.

To achieve this, however, our body needs numerous minerals and trace elements. However, if the buffer systems are overtaxed due to excessive acid levels, our body falls back on its own mineral deposits, which leads to dangerous demineralization. This mainly affects bones, teeth, nails, blood vessels, organs and the hair follicle.

The result is various diseases, such as osteoporosis, tooth decay, brittle fingernails, varicose veins, herniated discs and hair loss. This demineralization of the hair floor is only one of the many symptoms that can lead to serious diseases.

To prevent this process, it is important to restore the acid-base balance, remineralize the body and provide it with minerals on a permanent basis. (We will come to the subject of remineralization in detail later).

Therefore, one thing is clear: for a healthy organism, a balanced ratio of acids and bases is a very important factor.

A study by the "Center of Health" has shown that 100% of the participants who cleansed their bodies through deacidification and detoxification experienced stopped hair loss. [13] New hair growth even occurred in 90% of the subjects.

Deacidification in practice

The time to reverse acidity in the body depends on the duration and intensity of the acidity and can take one to three years. When you reach a value between 7 and 8 when testing with PH test strips, the first goal is achieved. The next goal should then be to maintain this ph level in the body. A sign that the body is back to normal is the feeling of vitality, happiness and general well-being.

When deacidifying, it is important to consume organic minerals that actually reach the cells. It is not enough if they are only present in the body, they must reach the cells. In addition, the mineral depots must be replenished to avoid recourse to minerals in the bones and tissues.

It is important to stick with deacidification and not get discouraged because it takes time. You shouldn't stop deacidifying after a few weeks and think it's not working. It is a process that takes time.

---

[13] p. 18, https://www.yumpu.com/de/document/read/7118067/haarausfall-studie-joico-onlineshop-vicopura (last call: 10.06.2023)

Methods for deacidification of the body

There are several methods to deacidify the body. Since the cause of hyperacidity may be different for each person and each person may react in an individual way to different methods, it would be best to consult a doctor or a qualified health advisor. Nevertheless, there are general recommendations that we will now discuss.

a) Nutrition

The decisive factor for deacidification is nutrition. For this we should know which foods are acidic and which are alkaline.

If you are striving to detoxify your body and keep your acid-alkaline balance in the healthy, alkaline range, it is important to minimize or avoid some acid-forming foods. These include meat and poultry, fish and seafood, dairy products, eggs, nuts, yeast products, white flour products, whole grain products, cereal products, carbonated beverages, refined fats and oils, margarine, legumes (all types of nuts except almonds), candy, black tea, coffee, alcohol and various canned foods.

Detoxifying foods such as garlic, citrus fruits, green vegetables, ginger and turmeric are especially good at deacidifying and detoxifying the body.

However, it is important to note that some of these acid-forming foods also contain important nutrients that are necessary for the body. Therefore, it is important to always consume them in conjunction with alkalizing foods and to respect a ratio of 20% acidifying to 80% alkalizing foods.

Active deacidification and maintenance of a healthy acid-base balance in the body can be supported by regular consumption of the following base-forming and alkaline foods:

Alkaline fruit: Apples, pineapples, apricots, avocado, bananas, pears, clementines, fresh dates, strawberries, figs, grapefruits, blueberries, raspberries, honey melon, currants, cherries, kiwis, limes, tangerines, mangoes, mirabeles, nectarines, olives, oranges, grapefruits, papayas, peaches, plums, cranberries, quinces, plums, gooseberries, star fruit, watermelons, grapes, lemons.

Alkaline vegetables / mushrooms: Eggplant, okra, oyster mushroom, bell pepper, celery, parsnip, cauliflower, parsley root, beans, green chanterelle, bovist, radicchio, broccoli, radish, mushroom, radish, cauliflower type, Chinese cabbage, alfalfa, lentils, amaranth, mung beans, buckwheat, rossabi, fennel seeds, red clover, arugula sesame seeds, millet, coriander seeds, Sunflower seeds, cress, wheat germ, flaxseed, beet, red cabbage, peas, shallots, fennel, salsify, spring onions, shiitake mushroom, kale, cucumber, carrot, porcini mushroom, potatoes, sweet potatoes, kohlrabi, pointed cabbage (sugar loaf), pumpkin, truffle mushroom, leek, white cabbage, chard, savoy cabbage, morel, zucchini, mu-err mushrooms, onions.

Alkaline salads and herbs: Basil, batavia lettuce, marjoram, savory, horseradish, nettle, lemon balm, watercress, nutmeg, Chinese cabbage, cloves, chicory, oregano, chili peppers, parsley, dill, pepper, oak leaf lettuce, peppermint, iceberg lettuce, allspice, endivem purslanem lamb's lettuce, radicchio, fennel seeds, romaine lettuce, frisee lettuce, rosemary, garden cress, arugula, ginger, saffron, capers, sage, cardamom, sorrel, chervil, chives, coriander, black cumin.[14]

---

[14] https://www.zentrum-der-gesundheit.de/krankheiten/haare/haarausfall-uebersicht/glatzenbildung
(last call: 09.06.2023)

Here are five important rules that you should definitely follow if you want to improve your hair growth in a direct way:

1. Don't drink alcohol

2. Avoid or reduce your sugar intake by refraining from consuming sweetened drinks. Instead, consider opting for sugar-free sweets available at organic stores.

3. Limit your consumption of caffeine by avoiding or minimizing the intake of caffeinated beverages such as coffee, cola, and other similar drinks.

4. Avoid consuming products made from white flour.

5. Start your day by drinking a large glass of warm water infused with freshly squeezed lemon in the morning (I will provide more details on this shortly). Additionally, aim to have your final meal of the day before 7 pm.

If you do all alone these five rules, you will soon feel a significant improvement in your well-being and performance. All five bad habits (alcohol, sugar, caffeine, white flour, late meals) stress, overacidify and slag your body. When you suddenly avoid them, your body breathes a sigh of relief. The less acids and waste products enter your body, the faster the old deposits - like in the hair floor - can be dissolved and eliminated. And that's the No. 1 prerequisite for new hair growth.[15]

---

[15] https://www.zentrum-der-gesundheit.de/krankheiten/haare/haarausfall-uebersicht/glatzenbildung (last call: 10.06.2023)

b) Hydration

One of the methods for deacidification is hydration or drinking water.

Hydration in the body refers to the process of water absorption and distribution in the body. Water is regulated by the kidneys and is used to keep the body hydrated and balance fluid levels.

When we drink, water enters the gastrointestinal tract and is absorbed by cells. It then supports the functions of organs and tissues, especially in regulating body temperature, lubricating joints and transporting nutrients.

If we do not take in enough water, dehydration can occur, which can manifest itself in symptoms such as fatigue, headaches and dry skin. To ensure adequate hydration, it is important to consume water and other hydrating fluids regularly.

With mild dehydration, short-term memory may be impaired, cognitive abilities may decline, and the skin may also age earlier. Additionally, we may experience cravings, fatigue, sleep disturbances and a more irritable mood. A lack of water intake also makes us more susceptible to possible infections, as our immune system is weakened.

It is of utmost importance to consume enough water to maintain physical and mental balance. Despite the trend towards healthy foods and so-called superfoods, we unfortunately don't know or forget that drinking water is just as important as a balanced diet (for example, it came back to me while writing these lines). But, of course, it is easier to reach for other sugary drinks instead of drinking water regularly. Therefore, we should make regular water drinking a program for us.

Experts recommend drinking about 200 ml of water as soon as you feel thirsty. But many people, especially the elderly, have a reduced sense of thirst and forget to drink regularly, which can lead to dehydration. A rule of thumb is to consume 30 ml of water per kilogram of body weight daily. This requirement can be increased during physical exertion such as sports or hard work.

Every morning lukewarm water

This is a separate book topic, but nevertheless I would like to address it here as briefly as possible because of its importance.

It is about Japanese water therapy. This is basically nothing more than drinking lukewarm or hot water in the morning. There are many studies about this. I link one of them in the footnote.[16]

Japanese water therapy can help activate the metabolism, flush toxins from the body, help build cells, protect against heartburn, and even help you lose weight. The heat activates the body, which leads to higher calorie consumption. Heat also facilitates the metabolism of subsequent food, which promotes better absorption of nutrients.

This water therapy is also considered a kind of detox. This is because the hot drink stimulates sweating and thus supports the elimination process of toxins through the skin. It also stimulates digestion and ensures adequate hydration, which is essential for efficient metabolism. Metabolism helps in the utilization, transformation and removal of useless substances from the body.

With the Japanese water cure, you can help your body fight and relieve various diseases. These include high blood pressure,

---

[16] https://archives.palarch.nl/index.php/jae/article/view/1407 (last call: 10.06.2023)

stomach problems, diabetes, constipation, gastritis and more. However, it is important to follow the cure for a certain period of time to achieve the desired effect. Here is an overview of the recommended period for some conditions:

- Hypertension- 30 days
- Stomach problems- 10 days
- Diabetes- 30 days
- Constipation- 10 days
- Gastritis- 10 days

The Japanese water diet will not only leave you with fewer cravings, but also with more radiant skin and shinier hair. Extra water can help your body cut down on unhealthy snacks and let you lose weight along the way. Adequate hydration also helps regenerate the skin and scalp, resulting in clear, glowing and toned skin and better hair growth. So it's worth trying out the simple Japanese water cure!

I would like to share with you another very interesting piece of information on this subject:

Warm water should also be beneficial for social skills, because it also positively affects your attitude. So not only will you be more attractive to other people, but you'll also be in a better mood. This is because the receptors in your mouth are directly connected to the pleasure center in your brain. When you drink warm water, these receptors are stimulated, which leads to awakening sympathy and friendliness for other people.

Avoid sparkling water, as carbon dioxide can irritate the stomach and trigger heartburn. Instead, prefer still mineral water or medicinal water with a high proportion of hydrogen carbonate.

It is recommended to drink the lukewarm water before brushing your teeth in the morning. Wait for at least 45 minutes before having breakfast, ideally allowing a two-hour gap before consuming any food.

As for the amount, it is recommended to drink 1 to 3 glasses of water (about 200 to 600 ml). If you prefer drinking lukewarm water, it will be easier for you to take in the recommended amount of fluid. Cold water can sometimes be uncomfortable, but lukewarm water is more pleasant to drink.

However, for those who do not like the taste, there is a simple solution: Refine it with a slice of fresh organic lemon. This gives the drink a tart flavor and provides additional vitamin C. In addition, the citrus makes the water anti-inflammatory. As an alternative, you can also add fresh mint or tea blossoms, but only after the water is no longer boiling hot. This way, the taste remains mild and hardly any bitter substances are added, which makes the drink more digestible on an empty stomach than many brewed teas.

Make it your daily habit to drink warm water in the morning and enjoy the many positive effects on your health.

c) Miracle Cure: Baking Soda

To deacidify my body, I used to use alkaline powder, which I stirred in water and drank. Later, however, I discovered baking soda as an alternative, which not only deacidifies the body, but also offers many other benefits and is also cheaper. I never imagined that such a home remedy, which is usually available in every household, could be such a great cure. These are not conspiracy theories, on the contrary, there are countless studies on this. Let's start.

Sodium hydrogen carbonate, often referred to simply as baking soda, is a substance that comes from nature. It was discovered around 1840 and at the beginning it was only used in bakeries, but later it was also used in many private households to prepare cakes and bread. The cleansing power of sodium bicarbonate and its ability to make flu and colds, as well as chronic diseases, disappear quickly was soon observed. This is due to the fact that soda has a high pH and is therefore alkaline.

People who are often ill and suffer from poor health tend to be over-acidic from a naturopathic point of view. This means that the pH of their tissues is not in the optimal range. However, according to the thesis of over-acidification and de-acidification, by consuming alkaline sodium bicarbonate, the over-acidity in the body can be neutralized and the pH levels can regulate.

With the rise of pharmaceutical drugs and the loss of personal responsibility for one's own health, interest in simple but effective remedies and aids waned. Doctors and their expensive prescriptions contributed to the disappearance of remedies like sodium bicarbonate, even though it was highly effective and free of side effects. But recently, even doctors have started to use sodium bicarbonate successfully in their cancer therapy, which shows that some things should not be forgotten and retain their value.

Now we come to the applications of sodium bicarbonate.

Application of sodium bicarbonate in cancer therapy

Recently, even orthodox medical researchers have discovered that sodium bicarbonate, or the bicarbonate it contains, can soften cancer tumors to such an extent that one can achieve much faster results with a much lower dose of chemotherapeutic agents (or radiation) than is normally the case. Therefore, one can bring these new findings to the attention of one's physician and possibly sodium bicarbonate will be used on oneself - in addition to chemotherapy.[17]

As early as 2009, Robert Gilles of the H. Lee Moffitt Cancer Center in Florida showed that, due to increased glucose metabolism, cancer thrives in a highly acidic environment, where metastases can form particularly well. However, when the patient (in this case a mouse) took sodium bicarbonate orally, the pH of the tumor tissue (in the experiment it was breast cancer) increased and the tumor became more alkaline.[18]

In May 2018, scientists at the Ludwig Institute for Cancer Research in New York revealed an intriguing mechanism of action that sodium bicarbonate can trigger in cancer, which may explain why it has such a high profile in folk medicine.[19]

Dr. Mark Sircus, a medical doctor, in his book "Sodium Bicarbonate: Rich Man's Poor Man's Cancer Treatment," describes the use of

---

[17] https://aacrjournals.org/cancerres/article/69/6/2260/552860/Bicarbonate-increases-Tumor-pH-and-Inhibits (last call: 10.06.2023)

[18] Gillies Ret al, Bicarbonate Increases Tumor pH and Inhibits Spontaneous Metastases, Cancer Research,March 2009.

[19] Ludwig Institute for Cancer Research, How might baking soda boost cancer therapy? Researchers describe how acidity turns oxygen-starved cancer cells dormant and drug resistant -- and a potentially easy way reverse the effect, ScienceDaily, June 1, 2018.

sodium bicarbonate as one of the cheapest, safest and most effective cancer drugs ever. Sodium bicarbonate can destroy cancer cells, according to Dr. Sircus, and is also used in traditional cancer therapy. Oncologists combine it with chemotherapy to protect vital organs from the toxic effects of chemotherapy. Dr. Sircus gives his patients sodium bicarbonate orally along with maple syrup and intravenously. He also recommends high doses of magnesium to aid in healing not only cancer, but many other diseases as well.

Dr. Tullio Simoncini, a controversial oncologist from Rome, injected sodium bicarbonate directly into tumor regions to "flush" them. He believed that taking sodium bicarbonate orally was only helpful for diseases that had spread to the digestive tract. Both scientists had good successes with their cancer patients, but also defeats. The latter is also common in traditional cancer therapy. Dr. Simoncini lost his license to practice medicine because of his sodium bicarbonate therapy and was convicted of manslaughter, among other things, because patients had died.

On the other hand, there are now many testimonials from people who have cured themselves with sodium, among other things. For example, Vernon Johnston of California, who was inspired by Dr. Mark Sircus, had prostate cancer and took sodium in conjunction with molasses. This measure was accompanied by other holistic methods, such as breathing exercises to increase oxygen intake. The cancer is said to have regressed on this. Another report comes from Käthe, who was diagnosed with Hodgkin's lymphoma at the age of 34 and took sodium along with other naturopathic methods.

The researchers led by Chi Van Dang, the institute's scientific director, discovered that cancer cells fall into an untreatable state when the surrounding tissue becomes increasingly depleted of oxygen and eventually becomes over-acidified. Especially in larger tumors, which are extremely low in oxygen and over-acidified, there are often accumulations of cancer cells that can hardly be reached by the usual cancer drugs and are therefore resistant to treatment.

Application in autoimmune diseases

As recently as April 2018, researchers announced that baking soda could create an anti-inflammatory environment in the body and thus could possibly be integrated into the therapy of autoimmune diseases.[20]

Soda has a unique ability to regulate and harmonize the immune system. By consuming soda water, changes in various immune cells have been observed in human subjects, including regulatory T cells that suppress autoimmune processes. This effect can be observed for at least four hours after drinking the soda water. Sodium bicarbonate is thus a safe way to treat inflammatory diseases with few side effects, Dr. O'Connor said.

Yes, the simple home remedy sodium bicarbonate dissolved in water can prove to be a real boon for our immune system. Researchers at Augusta University in Georgia, USA, have observed that after just a few weeks of taking such a drink, the immune system regulates and increases the number of anti-inflammatory defense cells, while the number of pro-inflammatory ones decreases. This anti-inflammatory effect could make natron a valuable support in the treatment of autoimmune diseases.[21] The results of their study were published in April 2018 in the prestigious

---

[20] Zandra E. Walton, Chi V. Dang et al, Acid Suspends the Circadian Clock in Hypoxia through Inhibition of TOR, Cell, May 31, 2018.

[21] https://www.sciencedaily.com/releases/2018/04/180425093745.htm (last call: 10.06.2023)

Journal of Immunology.[22]

Other areas of application

- Sodium hydrogen carbonate mouthwashes can be used to effectively combat bad breath while inhibiting the formation of tooth decay.

- Brushing teeth with sodium bicarbonate can also lead to brilliant white teeth, but this tip is only advisable if the enamel is perfect, as the powder can attack the enamel.

- A lemon water with baking soda can help against heartburn, but it should not be taken immediately before or after meals, because it can neutralize stomach acid and affect digestion. It is recommended to take the powder at least one hour before meals.

- Soda has many other uses, such as a home remedy for blackheads or as an important ingredient in alkaline baths. For more you can follow the link in the footnote.[23]

Application forms

Baking soda can be used in a variety of forms to help the body balance acid and alkaline. Here are some possibilities:

---

[22] Musall, Hiram Ocasio, Debra Irsik, Jessica A. Filosa, Jennifer C. Sullivan, Brendan Marshall, Ryan A. Harris, Paul M. O'Connor. Oral NaHCO3 Activates a Splenic Anti-Inflammatory Pathway: Evidence That Cholinergic Signals Are Transmitted via Mesothelial Cells. The Journal of Immunology, 2018; 1701605.

[23] https://www.zentrum-der-gesundheit.de/bibliothek/naturheilkunde/alternative-mittel/natron-gegen-chronische-entzuendung (last call: 10.06.2023)

1. Oral: Sodium bicarbonate can be taken in the form of tablets, capsules or powder. It is advisable to drink it with plenty of water to keep the body adequately hydrated.

2. Bathing: A bath with sodium bicarbonate can help to deacidify and relax the body, balance the acid-base balance in the body and relieve inflammation. Simply add one to two cups of the powder to a full bath and bathe for 20-30 minutes.

3. Inhalation: Some people also use sodium bicarbonate inhalation by putting it in a bowl of hot water and then inhaling it.

Benefits of sodium bicarbonate for hair

Soda has some benefits that can be beneficial for hair growth:

1. Balances pH: Soda can balance the pH of the scalp, which can promote hair growth and improve hair strength.

2. Removes dandruff: Soda can help remove dandruff, which can inhibit hair growth.

3. Cleanses the scalp: Soda has antiseptic properties and can help cleanse the scalp of excess oil and dirt, which can promote hair growth.

Ingesting baking soda: Things you need to know

If you're planning on taking baking soda, there are a few things to watch out for:

Make sure you use only the purest baking soda. It's readily and inexpensively available at supermarkets, drugstores or online, but make sure it's without additives (e.g. Kaiser baking soda). Don't confuse it with regular baking powder, although it can be used for some baking recipes. Conventional baking powder may also contain baking soda, but it also contains phosphate acidifiers, anti-caking agents, and possibly flavorings.

Personally, I can recommend this soda powder:

https://hawloo.eu/links/soda

Make sure you don't take it with meals, as it can neutralize important stomach acid and thus affect digestion. It is best to take it one hour before or two hours after a meal or before bedtime. Also, you should not take it with supplements so as not to neutralize their effect.

If you take baking soda regularly, you run the risk of manipulating the pH level of your stomach. Since the stomach needs a certain level of acidity to ensure smooth digestion, you shouldn't take too much of it. That's why it's generally recommended that you don't take baking soda in one piece for more than 30 days. After my research, I think the most beneficial form for me would be the following: After 30 days of continuous intake, the pH of the body is measured, and if it is not at the required alkaline level, another 30-day course could be done again after a break of one or two weeks. And again, if it is necessary, after the pH test was done, it can be continued again after 1-2 weeks break, and so on.

Excessive use of sodium carbonate can also stress the kidneys and cause electrolyte imbalances. It is therefore best to consult a doctor to determine if it is suitable for you. Especially during pregnancy, it is important to carefully discuss the use of sodium bicarbonate with your health care provider, as it may have an effect on the acid-base balance of your unborn child.

Also check if you are allergic to baking soda before taking it.

It can take one to three years to rid the body of hyperacidity. But you shouldn't stop deacidifying after just a few weeks because it takes time. Keep at it and don't get discouraged. Personally, I would, after each 30-day course of sodium bicarbonate, check my body's pH. If this value is between 7 and 8, I would take a break for 3-4 months. Otherwise, after a month, I would continue the cure until the optimal pH is reached.

Daily dose

Unfortunately, there is no scientifically based recommendation for your daily intake of sodium bicarbonate, which is associated with hair growth. Sodium bicarbonate is a salt that can be toxic in high doses, and overdosing can lead to health problems. Therefore, it is important that you stick to the recommended dosage that is stated on the product label and that you prefer to consult a doctor before starting. In fact, if you have a serious medical condition, it is imperative that you talk to your doctor before taking baking soda.

For example, my dear friend Nihat abi called an ambulance to his home one night because he had taken a little too much baking soda. As I learned later, he had used a dessert spoon instead of a teaspoon, probably hoping for a stronger effect. I still laugh when I think about it.

If you want to use bicarbonate of soda therapeutically, it is common practice to drink a glass of water (at least 120 ml) with about half a teaspoon of powdered bicarbonate of soda three times a day, for example, one hour before breakfast, one hour before lunch and two hours after a light and early dinner - preferably outside of meals, if you do not suffer from severe heartburn.

I myself take a teaspoon of bicarbonate of soda in my mouth only once a day before going to bed and mix it with water in my mouth before drinking it, instead of mixing it in a glass of water. I got this trick from my brother and friend Erdinç. This way, firstly, it is much easier for me and secondly, it has many other benefits. I read that in Japanese water therapy, you gargle with salt water for two minutes before going to bed. (This is basically the same thing I do, since baking soda is also a salt). This cleanses the mucous membranes and keeps the mouth and throat from becoming dry overnight. A dry mouth and throat provide ideal conditions for germs - and is the cause of bad breath in the morning. I also noticed that my teeth became whiter (or so I imagined). A fly massacre in one fell swoop. If you want to replicate this, be sure to drink another glass of water, as sufficient water is very important.

d) *Exercise and relaxation*

Maybe this part is self-evident for many, nevertheless I would like to address it briefly:

Regular physical activity and sports can be of great help in detoxifying and deacidifying the body. Exercise stimulates blood circulation and metabolism and helps the body eliminate harmful substances, keeping it balanced.

However, stress can contribute to hyperacidity and put a strain on the body. To avoid this, it is important to find relaxation methods. For example, meditation or progressive muscle relaxation are helpful here to relax and de-acidify the body. This can have a positive effect on physical and mental well-being.

2) PURIFICATION

In the past it was called purification, but today it is more commonly referred to as detox. In a modern detox cure, It is often sufficient to take a detox drink or a capsule on a daily basis. But a purification cure consists of many different measures and lasts several weeks.

The word "slag" refers to smelting residues in metal extraction and waste materials in the body that need to be eliminated.

Many doctors and scientists believe that the human body is good at detoxifying and purifying itself, without any extra help. But this is not always true; our bodies already have systems in place to rid themselves of toxins, but sometimes those systems don't work well. When that happens, it can cause physical discomfort. So it's important to support the body's own detoxification process. This is a smart way to heal the body and prevent disease.

It is now obvious that our bodies today cannot get rid of all the toxins and waste products we ingest. Studies show that we have hundreds of toxins stored in our blood, fat, skin, liver and digestive tract. Even in newborns, many chemicals have been found. Cigarettes and alcohol make it worse because they weaken our organs of elimination and take up their capacities. Therefore, it is important that we detoxify regularly to support our bodies.

Our current diet and lifestyle not only bring more waste, but it also contains too few nutrients. These nutrients (vitamins, minerals, antioxidants, phytochemicals and bitter substances) are necessary for the body to eliminate toxins. When we have too few of them, it becomes harder for the body to cleanse itself. If you study the subject of waste and toxin load, you will quickly realize how important it is to detoxify your body from time to time.

Consequences and symptoms of slagging

Slags are remnants of toxins and breakdown products from our diet, such as flavorings, preservatives and dyes. These are accumulate in our body and are deposited in cells, tissues and organs. Old, dead body cells can also accumulate as waste products. An unhealthy lifestyle and hyperacidity can lead to more slags accumulating in the body.

The body needs to get rid of acids and waste products to stay healthy. Normally, these are eliminated through our excretory organs. The body also disposes of them through other areas, such as:

- Hair floor and hair

- Whole skin

- Forehead

- Eyes (through tears)

- All mucous membranes

- Inside and outside of the nose

- Mouth and throat area

- Armpits

- Fingernails

- Hands

- Genitourinary tract

- Anus

- Lower leg

- Feet

- Toenails

When the body is overacidified, it tries to neutralize the acids and they are deposited in the body as slags. When the body is full of slags, it can lead to diseases. If there are too many slags in the hair base, it can lead to poor blood and nutrient supply, which causes the hair to fall out.

So if you are suffering from hair loss or other health problems, it may well be due to an excess of waste products in your body. Slags are simply what is left over when acids are produced in the body. So if you have less acids, you will have less waste products.

A vicious cycle:

When we eat wrong and load the body with environmental toxins, our body becomes overacidified. To neutralize the acids, our body takes minerals from the hair floor and other parts of the body. As a result, the hair weakens and falls out. The neutralized acids form slags, which slag the scalp and the rest of the body and lead to further hair loss.

To avoid this vicious circle, prevention is needed instead of cure later.[24]

Purification effect

---

[24] http://www.haarausfall-therapie.net/verschlackung-remineralisierung-entsaeuern/ (last call: 10.06.2023)

Purification seems like a panacea. It can even divide life into two parts: Before and after purification. Before, overweight, fatigue, lack of concentration, skin and digestive problems, pallor and illness prevail. After, you are slim, radiant, efficient and healthy. Purification is also recommended to fight chronic diseases or to recover from prolonged medication.

When you consider that our immune system is at the center of healthy intestinal flora and a healthy intestinal mucosa, and without a functioning immune system we can't stay healthy, it's hard to understand why some people call purging nonsense. Conventional medicine knows that cancer cells can be recognized and eliminated by a strong immune system. Regular detoxification can help maintain a strong immune system and thus prevent cancer. Autoimmune diseases often originate from a dysfunctional gut, so regular purges should be recommended. Unfortunately, many doctors discourage purges to protect their patients from fraud. However, this can be detrimental to their patients' health, chances of recovery, and lives.

Purification methods

There are very many purification methods. However, it is important to always discuss with a doctor or alternative practitioner before performing these methods. Here are some of them:

a) **Change in eating behavior**

If you want to detoxify the body, you should start with a change in diet. A healthy diet is important for the body to detoxify in the first place. So you should consume foods that help the body instead of burdening it. A good diet can also help the body detoxifying itself. It gives the body important nutrients, such as antioxidants that prevent damage from toxins and raw materials that the body needs to create detoxification enzymes and build new cells. This means that you don't have to fast during a detox to eliminate toxins. A few rules for a detoxifying diet:

- Buy fresh, seasonal and regional (ideally organic) food- Cook fresh and yourself
- Salads, vegetables and fruits should make up the majority of meals
- Supplement meals with easily digestible carbohydrates or proteins
- Drink plenty of water outside of meals

You can eat a lot of raw food, which is rich in vital substances and fiber and is good for detoxification. But make sure you chew the raw food well and eat it slowly so that it can be digested easily. If you don't tolerate raw foods well, you can turn to steamed and gently steamed dishes.

b) Deacidification

You can change the diet and at the same time also detoxify the body by deacidifying it. When cells are overacidified and clogged, they can no longer work normally and absorb nutrients or get rid of waste. To remove this blockage, we should deacidify our organism so that the cells can finally get rid of their toxins and waste and replenish themselves with nutrients. A good metabolism at the cellular level is important to successfully detoxify and stay healthy.

When you decide to detoxify your body, it is important to make a choice that fits your personal health. If you have been suffering from an illness or taking medication for a long time, it may be more difficult for you to do a strong deacidification diet. In this case, it is better to start with a gentler or medium strength deacidification diet, such as just a base concentrate or sodium bicarbonate in low doses.

I have already explained in detail how deacidification works and which deacidification methods exist, so have a look in the previous parts.

c) Gut Reset

Our intestine is part of our immune system and it is important for our health. When our immune system is weak, infections and diseases can occur. Skin problems and deficiencies in nutrient absorption can also be due to a disturbed intestinal flora. Therefore, it is important to keep the intestines clean and healthy. One can achieve this by cleansing the intestines. There are also special measures if one suspects parasites or a candida load. There are different types of colon cleanses, such as colonics or colon cleansing programs, that can be done at home. To go into detail here is beyond the scope of this book. But below in the footnote I provided a link for free instructions on how to do this.[25]

d) Purification of the lymph

When you cleanse your intestines, it is important to cleanse the

---

[25] https://www.zentrum-der-gesundheit.de/bibliothek/naturheilkunde/darmreinigung-uebersicht/darmreinigung (last call: 10.06.2023)

lymphatic system as well. The lymphatic system helps remove toxins from the body. You can incorporate lymph-cleansing activities such as exercise, massage, and herbal teas into your colon cleanse. If you don't cleanse the lymphatic system, congestion can occur and your detoxification and purification efforts can be compromised. The slower the lymphatic system works, the longer toxins stay in the body and can cause damage. See the footnote below for more details on this.[26]

e) Liver cleaning

If you have a clean and healthy intestinal flora, less toxins and wastes will enter the liver. Therefore, you should first cleanse the intestines before starting a liver cleanse. A cleansed intestinal flora can relieve the liver. Many adults have a fatty liver, either due to obesity or alcohol. An over-fat liver cannot perform its purpose as well and it can lead to a higher toxin load. It can also affect cholesterol levels. After completing the colon cleanse, it is time for a liver cleanse.

Cleansing the liver involves a diet rich in alkaline foods and certain ingredients such as bitters, milk thistle, artichoke extract, curcumin, capsaicin. This helps the liver function better and can show up in better liver values. For those interested, I link to two articles on this in the footnote.[27]

---

[26] https://www.zentrum-der-gesundheit.de/bibliothek/naturheilkunde/gesundheitskuren/lymphe-reinigen (last call: 10.06.2023)

[27] 1) https://www.zentrum-der-gesundheit.de/bibliothek/koerper/leber-und-galle/leberreinigung (last call: 10.06.2023)
2) https://www.zentrum-der-gesundheit.de/bibliothek/ratgeber/detox-uebersicht/pseudo-leberreinigung (last call: 10.06.2023)

f) Kidney detoxification

The kidneys are important for detoxification and purification of the body. When the intestines, lymphatic system and liver are healthy, the kidneys can work better. Therefore, before doing a kidney cleanse, you should do other detoxification methods. A kidney cleanse consists of herbs, water and foods that help the kidneys get rid of toxins. Herbs like nettle, dandelion, goldenrod, lovage, bearberry leaves, birch leaves, blackberry leaves and field horsetail can help in kidney cleanse.[28]

g) Detox cure or detoxification

Now that we have improved metabolism and cleansed all organs, the detoxification cure can begin. Even with the previous cleanses, some toxins have already been eliminated, but the most dangerous toxins are still active due to their difficulty to remove. Now all organs are ready to eliminate toxins more effectively and reduce the risk of re-poisoning. During a detox we can take specific measures to completely remove the fat-soluble toxins.[29]

Zeolite and bentonite are two minerals that can help rid the body of toxins. Zeolite is a volcanic earth and you can buy it as a powder and take it with water, usually about 5 grams a day, either all at once or divided into two intakes. It helps to bind toxins from the body and transport them out, also old toxins already deposited are gradually dissolved and removed. Bentonite is also recommended, but you should take it for a few weeks in addition to zeolite. After 4-5 weeks, one can then continue with zeolite only. A few days after taking

---

[28] https://www.zentrum-der-gesundheit.de/bibliothek/naturheilkunde/gesundheitskuren/nierenreinigung (last call: 10.06.2023)

[29] https://www.zentrum-der-gesundheit.de/bibliothek/ratgeber/detox-uebersicht/detox (last call: 29.03.2023)

zeolite, one can already feel an improvement in well-being, such as less fatigue and more freshness.

Here is a link to a good zeolite powder:

https://hawloo.eu/links/zeolite

h) Lemon juice cleansing cure

Freshly squeezed lemon juice is good for cleansing the body. It is used in various cleansing cures, such as the lemon juice cure according to Master Cleanse [30] or the lemon garlic cure [31]. The Master Cleanse is a type of fasting cure where you drink only diluted lemon juice with maple syrup and cayenne pepper. You normally do this for 3 to 10 days. You can do the lemon garlic cure besides your normal daily routine. You drink a glass of a special lemon garlic mixture every day. Start doing this for three weeks, then take a break for a week and start again for three weeks.

---

[30] https://www.zentrum-der-gesundheit.de/bibliothek/naturheilkunde/gesundheitskuren/master-cleanse (last call: 29.03.2023)

[31] https://www.zentrum-der-gesundheit.de/bibliothek/ratgeber/detox-uebersicht/zitronen-knoblauch-kur (last call: 29.03.2023)

i) Juice cure

Freshly squeezed juices taste great and help rid your body of unnecessary substances. Many people report living on juices alone and feeling better as a result. Juices are often an important part of healing fasting cures.

If you're looking for a juicer, I can recommend this one:

https://hawloo.eu/links/juicer

j) Health fasting

Therapeutic fasting is an ancient method of ridding the body of unwanted substances. There are two types of therapeutic fasting: Water fasting and Buchinger Fasting. In water fasting, you drink only water. Buchinger fasting involves drinking water, fresh juices and vegetable broth.

k) Alkaline fasting with alkaline foods

Alkaline fasting is a form of detoxification where you still eat solid food, but only from foods that are alkaline. It usually lasts two weeks and after that you should have a diet with more alkaline foods. It can also be taken as a preparation or follow-up for a water or Buchinger

Fasting.

If you need a detox planner, feel free to follow this link: https://bit.ly/3TOVlSb

Attention: Women should not perform purification cures during pregnancy or breastfeeding. Instead, it is recommended to plan a purification cure after breastfeeding. Sick people are strongly advised to discuss their plans for purification and dietary changes with a doctor or alternative practitioner, especially a fasting doctor.

3) REMINERALIZATION

When the old waste products or slags are gone, the nutrients and minerals that you supply with an alkaline diet and good supplements can get back into their place in the hair follicle. With proper care and nourishment, the previously neglected hair follicles will flourish and stimulate the growth of new hair.

The hair follicles could be compared to a small tree. If a tree does not receive enough light, water, and nutrients, then its growth slows down and it becomes more susceptible to diseases and pests. But just like a tree that is finally cared for, a hair follicle that is provided with the right resources can grow back to health and produce thick hair. This can be achieved through a hair loss or hair growth regimen, as well as a healthy diet and targeted supplements.

To make things more understandable, I would like to give another example: It's like a car. A car needs regular oil changes and fuel to run well. Just like a car, our body also needs regular nutrients and minerals. But when we eat unhealthy and live unhealthy, our body lacks what it needs. Our body then tries to make up for the deficit, but it can only do so for so long. If it goes without nutrients for too long, it becomes weaker and weaker. And just like a car that runs too long without oil and fuel, our bodies can break down. Metabolic acids and pollutants that we take in through unhealthy lifestyles, poor diets, and negative environmental influences put a strain on our bodies. A healthy body can easily eliminate these substances, but when our body is weak and over-acidified, it stores these substances. And if our body goes without nutrients for too long, it can lead to more serious health problems, not just hair loss. Therefore, it is important that we consume enough nutrients and minerals to keep our body and hair healthy.

Minerals are also important for us to neutralize acids and waste products in the body and to keep the pH value constant. This is very important because all processes in our body depend on a certain pH value. If we do not take in enough minerals through our food, they are drawn from the body's own mineral depots, which leads to acidification of the body. So to prevent hair loss, we need to consume enough minerals. If we do not supply the body with enough minerals, it will help itself to its own minerals. This can lead to a lack of important nutrients in the mineral balance. Since the base of the hair is the mineral depot that can be tapped most quickly, this is where nutrients are first depleted, leading to hair loss.

Advantages of remineralization

By avoiding the use of harmful chemicals and prioritizing the body's natural deacidification and purification processes, along with taking necessary natural supplements, we can achieve multiple benefits simultaneously. These supplements are so important because

1. this natural hair growth promotion is quite consistent.

2. they are not addictive, unlike the chemicals, and you can stop taking them when you want without having to fall back into the initial situation. However, it would be better if you always take some of them in certain sections over and over again.

3. they provide not only for the health of hair, but at the same time for the whole physical health.

4. in our modern society in the city we cannot always completely absorb the minerals and vitamins necessary for our body through diet, unless we live in the countryside, where we grow our own plants and our own animals on pasture.

5. according to my observation, successful people have also created a healthy life through nutritional means.

6. so that the problem will be solved to a large extent from the core.

The last point is the most important here. Because no matter what means you apply from the outside, the biggest problem should first be solved from the inside. That is, even if you apply certain lotions, shampoos, oils to the scalp or even do hair transplantation; if the problem is inside, that will only be a temporary solution. Therefore, in order to eliminate the hair problem entirely, one should approach the matter both from the inside (this is more important than the other) and from the outside.

Therefore, even the hair transplant is of no use if you do not solve the problem at the core, that is, inside. Because if the body suffers from vitamin and mineral deficiency and hyperacidity, it will not be able to supply the hair root, which will lead to hair loss early or late.

However, if you take the problem from the core, the hair roots will be properly supplied, which will eventually lead to natural hair growth. You will further learn that some supplements even create new hair roots (there are scientific studies on this). If you use these methods, you may not even need a hair transplant.

Demineralization of the hair floor

According to Dr.h.c. Peter Jentschura, hair growth indicates the state of the body's neutralization potential.[32] Most naturopathic and complementary doctors are convinced that hair loss is primarily a problem of mineral depletion in the scalp due to acid neutralization.

Our body has various buffer systems to compensate for hyperacidity. Blood, lungs, tissues, intestines and kidneys are among them. When acidity exceeds these natural buffers, our body looks for substances that can bind and neutralize excess acids: Minerals.

A constant pH value in the blood between 7.35 and 7.45 is vital, as a deviation can lead to acute, life-threatening problems. If our body becomes overacidified and is not sufficiently supplied with minerals through our diet, it has to fall back on its own reserves. In doing so, it goes where it can tap the nutrients most quickly.

The most readily accessible mineral depot is the hair floor, followed by the roots of the teeth. The body extracts minerals from the scalp to keep the pH value constant but the hair needs this to grow and develop. This causes the hair to fall out. Men are more often affected than women because women have an effective deacidification mechanism through their menstruation. This also explains why people (especially men) first lose their hair with age, then their teeth.

Dr.h.c. Peter Jentschura and Josef Lohkämper refer to this disease, in which minerals are withdrawn from the body, as "civil isatosis". They believe that the demineralization of our body not only leads to hair loss, but can also be responsible for a variety of diseases. These

---

[32] p. 4, https://www.probiosa.de/wp-content/uploads/Ratgeber_wie_entschlacke_ich_erfolgreich_D_11-2012_V-0107-2011_web.pdf (last call: 10.06.2023)

include tooth decay, high blood pressure, periodontal disease, osteoporosis, arteriosclerosis (hardening of the blood vessels), varicose veins, intervertebral disc disease, hernias, foot sweat, dental plaque, ulcerated tonsils, eczema, boils, carbuncles, neurodermatitis, allergies, psoriasis, open leg, skin itching, hemorrhoids, gallstones, kidney stones, bladder stones, rheumatism, gout, arthrosis, stroke, tartar, lipomas, fibromas, dyslexia, diabetes mellitus, gastritis, ulcerative colitis, Parkinson's disease, Alzheimer's disease, arthritis, Crohn's disease and Bechterev's disease.

Methods for remineralization of the body

To prevent mineral deficiency and rebalance the body, there are numerous methods of remineralization. Here you can resort to natural and uncomplicated methods, such as a balanced diet and the consumption of mineral-rich foods but also to targeted supplements. Below I will share a variety of methods to remineralize the body to help you rebalance your body and promote healthy, strong hair.

a) Vitamin P (OPC)

Let's start first with OPC, which is considered one of the most important vitamins.

OPC or vitamin P is a relatively new vitamin that is often hidden because of its powerful effects. There are not many studies about OPC but the available studies show very positive effects on our health.

OPC is a nutrient of great importance for our health. Despite decades of research by renowned professors around the world, all of which attest to amazing positive effects on health, OPC is still not officially recognized and just a few people know its benefits.

It is scandalous that this important nutrient is not known despite its importance. However, thanks to the Internet, it is possible to obtain information on OPC and there are also already some recommended books on this subject on the market as well as scientific studies, which I will link as a footnote.

OPC is an abbreviation for Oligomeric Proanthocyanidins, also known as oligomeric procyanidins or proanthocyanidin complexes. OPC's are plant compounds found in various foods such as grape seeds, pine bark, red wine, berries, and cocoa. They belong to a group of compounds known as flavonoids, which are known for their antioxidant properties and positive effects on health.

Everyone needs OPC and can benefit enormously from a sufficient supply. Unfortunately, OPC is almost completely banned from our diet due to modern food processing, long storage times and other factors. Many people suffer from vitamin deficiency, which is a major health problem. The amount of vitamins and nutrients in our fruits and vegetables is constantly decreasing due to depleted soils, air pollution and rapid growth. Therefore, vitamin deficiency should be compensated by high-quality natural supplements. It is also available as a dietary supplement in capsule form.

OPC and Vitamin C & Co.

OPC is the most powerful antioxidant known in the world and many experts consider it the new vitamin C. OPC can prolong and enhance the effectiveness of vitamins. Studies show that vitamins C, A and E remain active ten times longer in the presence of OPC. [33] Only 11% of men and 14% of women reach the recommended amount of vitamin C. OPC is quickly absorbed by the body and is detectable in the blood after only a few minutes after its consume.

In summary, OPC, together with vitamin C, is involved in almost all processes in the body and the two nutrients complement and reinforce each other perfectly, which makes them the most important substances after oxygen and water for the human body.

OPC and Anti-Aging

OPC can slow down aging and be a cause for a long life.[34] Scientists say that it is the most powerful antioxidant we know. It fights free radicals in the body that destroy cells and accelerate aging. In animal studies, it has been shown that taking OPC "prolonged" the lives of animals by an average of 30% to 40%. According to molecular researchers, if we start taking OPC early, we can live up to 120 years

---

[33] p. 10, Werner Goller, "What Does Conventional Medicine Conceal?" 2009.

[34] p. 68, Anne Simons, Alexander Rucker "Healthy living longer through OPC" 2005.

or more. The average life expectancy of a human is 77 years, but with the extension of 40%, we could live 108 years. So OPC helps to slow down the biological age.[35]

OPC and Skin Health

Since OPC is 18 to 20 times more potent than vitamin C and even 40 to 50 times more potent than vitamin E, it offers countless benefits for our skin as well.

OPC can prevent skin aging and wrinkles and smooth already existing wrinkles. This happens due to three mechanisms:

1. Regulation of the sprouting of collagen

2. Enhancement of the effect of vitamin C for strong collagen formation

3. Protection of collagen and elastin from attack by aggressive enzymes

A study by the Unilever Research Institute in the United Kingdom observed 4000 women over the age of 40 and found that those women who consumed more vitamin C had fewer wrinkles.

OPC is already an effective anti-aging agent on its own, but together with vitamin C, the effect is enhanced.

Furthermore, OPC has the potential to revitalize the skin and offer protection against the harmful effects of UV radiation, akin to a

---

[35] https://www.sciencedirect.com/science/article/abs/pii/S0300483X00002109?via%3Dihub
(last call: 29.03.2023)

sunscreen.[36]

Since OPC promotes the building of collagen, it can thus accelerate the healing of wounds[37] and prevent the appearance of acne.

OPC and Hair Growth

OPC and vitamin C have not only many positive effects on our body. They are hormonal, antiviral and antibacterial. In addition, they cleanse, are antioxidant and support the building of collagen and elastin. Maintaining a healthy scalp and hair requires precisely the antioxidant and supportive effects of collagen and elastin building.

There are unfortunately limited scientific studies for the effect of OPC on hair growth. However, some small studies and laboratory experiments have shown that OPCs may have potential benefits for hair health, including:

- Promoting hair growth by increasing the blood supply to the scalp and improving the supply of nutrients and oxygen to the hair follicles.

- Reduction of inflammation associated with hair loss.

- Protecting hair follicles from damage caused by free radicals and UV radiation.

- Promoting the growth of healthy, radiant and rapidly regrowing hair

Studies from Japan have shown that OPC can increase the cell

---

[36] https://onlinelibrary.wiley.com/doi/10.1111/jocd.13711 (last call: 29.03.2023)

[37] https://www.ccsenet.org/journal/index.php/gjhs/article/view/40015 (last call: 29.03.2023)

proliferation of hair follicles by 230% compared to other preparations. In addition, OPC affects the hair cycle and increases the number of hairs in the growth phase.[38] I must also mention that these results are preliminary and further studies are needed to confirm the effectiveness of OPCs for hair growth.

However, it is clear that OPC from grape seed extract is considered a recommended component for promoting hair growth.

Other advantages of OPC

Adequate daily intake of OPC may have several health benefits due to the antioxidant and anti-inflammatory properties of these compounds.

OPC enhances the effect of vitamins C, E and A and can regulate the production of histamine and histidine, resulting in fewer allergies and improved symptoms of allergic reactions. OPC has anti-inflammatory and anti-asthmatic effects and can thus improve or even prevent the course of the disease.

OPC also has a strong antioxidant effect, which it has a protective effect on all cells of the human body and improves the body's defenses.

Within just 24 hours of the initial intake, the resistance of blood vessels can double, and with continued use, it may even triple. This is especially important for people who have an increased risk of strokes, as it can prevent blood from clumping together and blood vessels from remaining elastic.

---

[38] https://pubmed.ncbi.nlm.nih.gov/9833041/ (last call: 29.03.2023)

OPC can relieve depression, winter mood and daytime fatigue. It can also improve cognitive function and memory, increase concentration and intelligence, and prevent impotence. It can also relieve menstrual problems and increase fertility.

OPC strengthens the gums, protects the lungs and helps prevent osteoporosis. OPC improves blood circulation and can thus prevent heavy legs and lymphatic congestion. It can also prevent eye problems[39] such as cataracts[40] and make the skin more supple.

Studies show that OPC from grape seed extract can inhibit the growth of cancer cells[41] such as breast, colon and lung cancer.[4243] It is also being discussed whether OPC can help as an adjunctive therapy in chemotherapies[44] to minimize side effects. In one study, South African researchers showed that grape seed extract with OPC and other active ingredients can kill cancer cells in colorectal cancer[45] while leaving healthy cells unaffected.[46]

OPC can help with collagen and elastin synthesis, which means it helps build and repair our body tissues. It can also neutralize free radicals, with 20 times more effect than vitamin C and 50 times more effect than vitamin E.[47]

Arteriosclerosis is a calcification of arteries that causes the blood to

---

[39] https://www.ncbi.nlm.nih.gov/pmc/articles/PMC3025097/ (last call: 29.03.2023)

[40] https://link.springer.com/article/10.1007/s12603-014-0020-8 (last call: 29.03.2023)

[41] https://academic.oup.com/carcin/article/20/9/1737/261642?login=false (last call: 29.03.2023)

[4242] https://aacrjournals.org/cancerpreventionresearch/article/12/8/557/47242/A-Pilot-Study-of-a-Grape-Seed-Procyanidin-Extract (last call: 29.03.2023)

[43] https://www.ncbi.nlm.nih.gov/pmc/articles/PMC3622127/ (last call: 29.03.2023)

[44] https://aacrjournals.org/clincancerres/article/12/20/6194/191679/Grape-Seed-Extract-Inhibits-In-vitro-and-In-vivo (last call: 29.03.2023)

[45] https://www.sciencedirect.com/science/article/abs/pii/S0304383507004037?via%3Dihub (last call: 29.03.2023)

[46] https://link.springer.com/article/10.1007/s13197-019-04113-w (last call: 29.03.2023)

[47] https://pubmed.ncbi.nlm.nih.gov/9090754/ (last call: 29.03.2023)

not flow properly. When the artery is clogged, the heart cannot get oxygen and heart attacks can occur. If the brain does not get oxygen, it leads to a stroke. Pulmonary infarction and thrombosis are also consequences of arteriosclerosis. Unfortunately, 50% of all people in Central Europe die from this mechanism, but OPC can be a cause to stop it – even reverse it.

Overall, OPC offers many benefits to the body, from improving health to preventing and fighting disease.

The right dose

For healthy people, it is recommended to take 3 mg of OPC per kg of body weight for the first 14 days, after which you can reduce to 2-3 mg per kg of body weight and maintain this amount. Consistent consumption of OPC throughout life is essential for sustaining its health benefits.

When OPC is used to treat disease, dosages of 400mg or more daily are often administered without any interactions or side effects. These dosages have been used in the treatment of varicose veins, retinal disease, osteoarthritis, PMS, sports injuries, and postoperative edema.[48]

Important for the intake of OPC

When you take OPC or vitamin P for the first time, it may initially cause some unpleasant symptoms such as headaches, fatigue, flu-like symptoms or malaise. This is because by taking OPC, toxins such as heavy metals, pesticides and herbicides are eliminated from the

---

[48] p. 10, Anne Simons, Alexander Rucker "Healthy living longer through OPC" 2005.

body more quickly.

But don't worry, these symptoms are a good sign and usually disappear after a few days. The stronger the symptoms were, the better you will feel afterwards. Green tea can be supportive and help your body detoxify. So don't get discouraged and continue taking OPC, you will soon feel fitter and healthier!

When taking OPC, it is recommended to take it half an hour before or after a meal. Since it is stored in the body for 72 hours, taking it once a day is sufficient. But be careful not to take it with protein-rich foods such as dairy products or eggs, as it may bind to them instead of your own protein in the body. If you take larger amounts of OPC, especially in combination with vitamin C, you should also remember to deacidify your body by taking bases.

OPC or vitamin P has no known harmful side effects. A study with a high dosage of OPC over a period of six months showed no adverse effects. In France, OPC is a component of three vasoprotective medications and has been successfully prescribed for a long time. OPC has also been found to be as safe as vitamin C.[49]

There are two reasons why you might want to avoid OPC capsules. First, one should not take OPC capsules if one is taking blood thinning medications, as both can affect blood thinning. Secondly, one should avoid OPC capsules if one is allergic to grapes, as OPC capsules are made from grape seed extract. It is important to consider one's allergies and medications before taking OPC capsules.

When you buy OPC as a dietary supplement, it is important to pay attention to the quality. It should have a content of at least 95% OPC and be labeled as "OPC 95". If this is not indicated, it may be a lower

---

[49] p. 10, Anne Simons, Alexander Rucker "Healthy living longer through OPC" 2005.

quality with only 40% OPC content.

It is also important that enough grape extract is included. A good amount would be 525mg per package, which is about 250 mg per capsule. There are also other important ingredients like vitamin C, E and beta-carotene that should be included. You should avoid controversial and dangerous additives like magnesium stearate.

Despite this, it is always advisable to consult with a physician or nutritionist before taking OPCs as a dietary supplement.

I find these capsules the best by price-performance ratio:

https://hawloo.eu/links/opc

OPC - make facial tonic yourself.

As OPC supports collagen and elastin synthesis, it improves cosmetic appearance by promoting cell regeneration. Therefore, you can combine it with cleansing toner or body oil lotion for even better results. For this, you only need two simple ingredients: OPC capsules and rose water:

1. Open one capsule of OPC and dissolve the powder in rose water.

2. Shake the mixture and soak a cotton ball in it.

3. Clean your face with the soaked cotton ball.

It's that easy to make your own OPC facial toner!

b) Vitamin C

OPC and vitamin C are considered perfect partners, so I would continue directly with vitamin C.

Before I got involved with vitamin C, I would never have thought that vitamin C was a real multi-talent.

In earlier times, the human body was capable of endogenously synthesizing vitamin C. However, while many animals still retain this ability, humans have lost it over time. Why, is unclear, but it could be because there was enough vitamin C in nature. Interestingly, animals that produce vitamin C themselves produce much more than we take in through our food. Linus Pauling concluded that our need for vitamin C is much higher than we think and that we need more of it than we get from an apple and a few lettuce leaves a day. We'll get to how much we need later.

Vitamin C = Ascorbic Acid?

Vitamin C and ascorbic acid are often the same thing, but there are subtle differences. Vitamin C is actually a specific form of ascorbic acid, more specifically L-ascorbic acid. There are other forms of ascorbic acid, such as dehydroascorbic acid, that are found in foods and can be converted to L-ascorbic acid in the body. But there are also ascorbic acids that have no vitamin C effect, such as D-ascorbic acid, which is used in foods as a preservative. In short, vitamin C is a kind of ascorbic acid, but not all ascorbic acid is vitamin C.[50]

Functions of Vitamin C

---

[50] https://lpi.oregonstate.edu/mic/vitamins/vitamin-C (last call: 29.03.2023)

Vitamin C has many important tasks in the body. Many people know it as a protection against colds. But vitamin C has many other important functions:

- Strengthens the immune system.

- Protects against free radicals as an antioxidant

- Strengthens the connective tissue

- Protects the vessels

- Improves the absorption of calcium and iron

- Important for certain hormones

- Detoxifies the body

Vitamin C and Diseases

Vitamin C helps strengthen the immune system and protects the body from disease. Orthomolecular physicians say that vitamin C can help with many diseases related to inflammation in the body. These include allergies, heart disease, cancer, autoimmune diseases and more.[51]

Heart Disease and Vitamin C

Heart disease is one of the most common causes of death in Germany. Sometimes, narrowed blood vessels can occur due to deposits in the vessels. If a blood vessel is completely blocked, it can lead to a heart attack, stroke or other organ infarction. Researchers have found that people who eat lots of fruits and vegetables and

---

[51] https://pubmed.ncbi.nlm.nih.gov/29099763/ (last call: 10.06.2023)

have high levels of vitamin C in their blood have a 15% lower risk of heart disease. It could also be that a vitamin C deficiency is a cause of heart disease.[52]

Vitamin C and Hair Growth

Vitamin C is beneficial for hair growth because it supports the following functions:

1. Promote blood circulation: Vitamin C can improve blood circulation in the head and hair area, which can help nutrients and oxygen reach the hair roots.

2. Support collagen production: Vitamin C is important for the production of collagen, an important building block of hair. Sufficient collagen production can help keep hair healthy and strong.

3. Protection against oxidative stress: Vitamin C is an antioxidant that protects the body from oxidative stress. This oxidative stress can damage the hair follicles, which can lead to hair loss and slow hair growth.

4. Support thyroid function: Vitamin C can support the function of the thyroid gland, which is important for hair growth.

The Dose of Vitamin C

---

[52] https://pubmed.ncbi.nlm.nih.gov/28338764/ (last call: 10.06.2023)

It is well known that vitamin C is essential for life. The optimal daily intake of vitamin C is a subject of ongoing debate and discussion. According to official information, one should only take about 100 mg of vitamin C per day. Orthomolecular physicians maintain that this amount is insufficient.[53]

For people who are ill, there are no precise recommendations for the daily vitamin C requirement. However, it is assumed that their requirement is higher than that of healthy people.[54] This is because illness is often accompanied by vitamin C deficiency, due to a lower intake of food from the illness and a higher need for vitamin C due to oxidative stress. Studies have shown that a higher intake of vitamin C can shorten the time patients have to spend in an intensive care unit.

Why orthomolecular physicians call for higher doses of vitamin C?

Our diet has changed greatly over the centuries. Due to advances in the food industry, we probably consume less vitamin C today than in the past. Many amounts of vitamin C are lost through the transportation, storage and processing of food. However, our diets used to contain more fresh fruits and raw vegetables. Therefore, our daily vitamin C requirement may actually be higher than it is currently estimated.

In addition, people today are exposed to many environmental stresses that can lead to oxidative stress. These include stress, pesticides in food, chemicals in personal care products, air pollution, X-rays and surgery. All of this increases the need for antioxidants.

---

[53] https://pubmed.ncbi.nlm.nih.gov/26227083/ (last call: 10.06.2023)

[54] https://www.ncbi.nlm.nih.gov/pmc/articles/PMC6835439/ (last call: 10.06.2023)

Vitamin C is an important part of this to keep the body healthy. As we are exposed to more environmental stresses today, it may be necessary to take more vitamin C to prevent disease.

Orthomolecular medicine is concerned with studying deficiencies in important nutrients and recommending nutrients for disease prevention. The German Society for Orthomolecular Medicine (DGOM) thinks the recommended daily vitamin C requirement is far too low: "No wonder toddlers have colds all the time. That wasn't the case 50 years ago," it writes on its website. [55] The DGOM suggests the following daily doses:

- Newborn: 50 mg
- 1st year of life: 30 mg per kg body weight, increasing to 500-1000 mg by the end of the first year of life.
- **2nd year of life until end of life: 50-100 mg per kg body weight**
- Nursing mothers: at least 2000 mg of vitamin C per day

According to the DGOM, a person weighing 60 kg should therefore consume 3000-6000 mg of vitamin C per day - at a weight of 80 kg this would be 4000-8000 mg. These values are of course very high compared to the officially recommended daily requirement. However, animals that produce vitamin C themselves can produce 500 mg to over 20 g of vitamin C per day. Therefore, the officially recommended daily intake of 100 mg for humans seems somewhat low. Probably a compromise between the official requirement and the amounts recommended by the DGOM is the best option, for example 500-1000 mg of vitamin C per day for a healthy adult.

---

[55] https://www.dgom.de/wissenswertes/kompendium/lebensnotwendige-molekuele/ascorbin (last call: 29.03.2023)

Vitamin C Deficiency

A prolonged deficiency of vitamin C is known as scurvy and is fatal.[56] It is a disease that used to be common among sailors who were at sea for long periods of time and did not have fresh foods with vitamin C. Today, scurvy has become rare, but there are still many people who don't get enough vitamin C. You can avoid scurvy by taking at least 10 mg of vitamin C a day.[57]

Causes of vitamin C deficiency

- Inadequate diet, which contains little vitamin C[58]

- Smoking, passive smoking, alcohol and drug abuse, which lead to more oxidative stress

- Medication use such as birth control pills, antibiotics, diuretics, and aspirin.

- Serious diseases such as cancer[59], severe kidney disease, cachexia[60]

- Gastrointestinal diseases that damage the mucosa in the small intestine and impair nutrient absorption

High environmental exposures prolonged vitamin C deficiency may contribute to the development of chronic diseases [61] such as

---

[56] https://pubmed.ncbi.nlm.nih.gov/8692035/ (last call: 29.03.2023)

[57] https://pubmed.ncbi.nlm.nih.gov/19508394/ (last call: 29.03.2023)

[58] https://pubmed.ncbi.nlm.nih.gov/12134712/ (last call: 29.03.2023)

[59] https://pubmed.ncbi.nlm.nih.gov/3917362/ (last call: 29.03.2023)

[60] https://pubmed.ncbi.nlm.nih.gov/12771534/ (last call: 29.03.2023)

[61] https://ods.od.nih.gov/factsheets/VitaminC-Consumer/ (last call: 29.03.2023)

osteoarthritis and autoimmune diseases, and may also be associated with Alzheimer's disease and depression.[62]

Symptoms of vitamin C deficiency

A mild deficiency can show up as weakness, fatigue, muscle pain, reduced performance and increased susceptibility to infections. Unfortunately, individuals often fail to seek medical attention for these seemingly inconsequential symptoms, resulting in the undiagnosed deficiency. A severe deficiency, known as scurvy, can lead to bleeding, brown, scaly and dry skin, poor wound healing, loose teeth and joint pain. Long-lasting vitamin C deficiency can also contribute to atherosclerosis and cardiovascular disease.[63]

Identification of vitamin C deficiency

A blood test can be taken to determine whether or not an individual is deficient in vitamin C. This is done at the doctor's office and helps determine the amount of vitamin C in the body. Normally, values between 3 and 14 mg per liter of blood are good, but depending on the laboratory, these reference values can vary. If the levels are below 1.7 mg per liter of blood, it may mean that you have a vitamin C deficiency. If the levels are very low, below 1 mg per liter of blood, there is even a risk of a disease called scurvy. However, it is difficult to tell if one has a deficiency because the symptoms are often

---

[62] https://www.ncbi.nlm.nih.gov/pmc/articles/PMC6071228/ (last call: 29.03.2023)

[63] p. 119-129, Price, K. D., Price, C. S. C., & Reynolds, R. D. (1996). Hyperglycemia-induced latent scurvy and atherosclerosis: The scorbutic-metaplasia hypothesis. Medical Hypotheses, 46(2).

inconspicuous and are not always detected.[64]

To avoid vitamin C deficiency, one should consume more than the recommended amount. An official daily requirement of 100 mg of vitamin C can easily be achieved by eating two oranges, but as mentioned earlier, experts believe that this requirement is underestimated today. Therefore, it may be helpful to consume higher doses of vitamin C to avoid deficiency.

Types of vitamin C

It's best to get as much vitamin C as you can from fruits and vegetables, as they also contain other important nutrients.[65] Here are some foods that contain a lot of vitamin C. When you get the vitamin C from fruits and vegetables, it is present along with other ingredients and your body can use it better. However, according to experts in orthomolecular medicine, these days you can't get the recommended amount of vitamin C from diet alone. Therefore, higher amounts must be supplied through supplements.

There are many different types of vitamin C supplements:

1.   With natural vitamin C, such as from acerola cherries or camu camu

2.   With pure ascorbic acid, which can also be of natural origin

3.   With buffered vitamin C

64

https://www.mlhb.de/fileadmin/user_upload/Startseite/Service/Laborinformationen/Vitamin_C_0216.pdf (last call: 29.03.2023)

[65] https://www.zentrum-der-gesundheit.de/pdf/tabelle_lebensmittel_mit_vitamin_c.pdf (last call: 29.03.2023)

4. Vitamin Ester-C®

5. Ascorbyl palmitate

6. Liposomal Vitamin C

It is best to take vitamin C supplements (except liposomal vitamin C) in 3 to 6 small doses throughout the day. But if that is not possible, it is still better to take one dose in the morning and one in the evening rather than all at once. Vitamin C supplements are available in the form of tablets, effervescent tablets, powder or lozenges. Powder is the best choice because it's easiest to divide into smaller doses and customize the amount you want. You simply mix the powder with water and drink it. Effervescent tablets can also be drunk with water. Tablets and lozenges are more suitable for on the go, when you don't have water with you. But beware: Effervescent tablets and lozenges often contain additives such as sweeteners, acidifiers, artificial flavors and sometimes even sugar. It is better to choose pure powder or capsules. Pure ascorbic acid is better tolerated if taken after meals. Otherwise, gastrointestinal problems may occur, depending on individual tolerance.

Vitamin C overdose

Is it harmful to take very high doses of vitamin C? Since vitamin C is water-soluble and excess is excreted in the urine, there is little chance of harm. However, if you take too much ascorbic acid at one time, it can cause gastrointestinal symptoms such as diarrhea. How sensitive everyone is to an overdose varies. Vitamin C from fruits and vegetables is better tolerated, but you can't take such high doses of it.

In principle, taking high doses of ascorbic acid is safe, whether orally or intravenously. When comparing the symptoms of an illness or the side effects of medications with the risk of temporary diarrhea, the decision is easy for some. [66]

But still, before you take high-dose vitamin C, pay attention to whether any of the following apply to you.

Side effects of vitamin C

Vitamin C can interact with certain drugs and affect their action. Since vitamin C is an acid, it can chemically alter other active ingredients. For example, it may interfere with the excretion of acetylsalicylic acid (e.g., aspirin), decrease the effect of blood-thinning anticoagulants, and decrease the concentration of fluphenazine in the blood. It is important to talk to your doctor before taking high-dose vitamin C supplements if you are taking any medications.

People with iron storage disease (hemochromatosis) should not take supplements with vitamin C, because vitamin C promotes iron absorption. In this case, vitamin C should be taken only in consultation with the doctor.

It has been discussed that the intake of vitamin C can lead to kidney stones, especially when more than 1000 mg are taken daily. However, the study situation on this is not clear. A causal relationship is not known worldwide.

Half of all kidney stones consist of calcium phosphate, magnesium ammonium phosphate or calcium carbonate. These form when the urine is alkaline (basic). If you take vitamin C, you can prevent the stones from forming. The other half of kidney stones are made of

---

[66] https://www.dgom.de/wissenswertes/kompendium/lebensnotwendige-molekuele/ascorbin (last call: 29.03.2023)

calcium oxalate, urate or cystine and form when the urine is acidic. In this case, one should take either sodium ascorbate or ascorbic acid together with the same amount of soda or natron (sodium bicarbonate).[67]

The best vitamin C

I have done a lot of research and have come to the conclusion that the best and safest vitamin C food is the natural vitamin C from acerola cherries. My personal opinion is absolutely based on my own research.

---

[67] https://www.dgom.de/wissenswertes/kompendium/lebensnotwendige-molekuele/ascorbin (last call: 29.03.2023)

To make it easier for you, I would like to share my favorite article on this:

https://hawloo.eu/links/vitaminc

If that is too much trouble for you and you prefer to take it in capsule form, I can recommend the following. But because in this article the dose of a capsule is only 80 mg, I find it a bit insufficient; unless you take several capsules a day. But that would be more elaborate for me than the previous one:

https://hawloo.eu/links/vitaminc-cpsl

c) *Vitamin D*

Allow me to preface by mentioning that I prioritize vitamin intake based on its significance in promoting hair growth, rather than adhering to alphabetical order. Whereby the priority may vary from person to person.

In connection with this, we come to vitamin D.

Vitamin D is a fat-soluble vitamin and can be stored in the body. There are mainly two forms of vitamin D: Vitamin D2 and vitamin D3. It is true that mostly vitamin D3 is considered the better vitamin D, while vitamin D2 is not supposed to work as well. Therefore, there are hardly any supplements with vitamin D2.

Vitamin D is one of the vitamins that are soluble in fat, just like vitamins A, E and K. This has two meanings:

- To absorb vitamin D from food, we also need some fat

- Vitamin D can be stored in the body (in fatty tissue and in the liver). This is almost never the case with water-soluble vitamins (B, C)

The advantage is that you do not have to eat vitamin D every day once the stores are full. The body can even live off these stores for weeks or months. But this also means that you can take too much of these vitamins. While too much of water-soluble vitamins is simply excreted in the urine, this is not the case with fat-soluble vitamins.

Advantages of vitamin D

Vitamin D has many important functions in the body and offers the following benefits:

- Support bone growth and strength: Vitamin D helps the body absorb and use calcium, which is essential for bone growth and strength. It keeps bones healthy and can prevent osteomalacia, osteoporosis and falls with fractures.

- Immune system support: Vitamin D supports the immune system by helping to fight infections and diseases and protects against infections, allergies and tumors.

- Regulation of calcium metabolism: Vitamin D helps the body balance calcium in the blood, which is essential for healthy heart and muscle function and for healthy nervous system function.

- Promoting Mental Health: Vitamin D is often associated with improved mood and mental health, studies have shown that vitamin D can play an important role in regulating mood and that a deficiency of vitamin D can be associated with depression.

- Muscle and body coordination: Vitamin D is important for muscle function and body coordination.

- It is good for the nervous system and can prevent multiple sclerosis and dementia.

- It is important for balanced hormones and can prevent diabetes.

- A study has shown that vitamin D also protects against colds and other acute respiratory infections.[68] People with low vitamin D levels have a higher risk of developing covid-19.[69]

- Many studies confirm this view and show that vitamin D can reduce cancer growth. 15 different types of cancer are associated with low vitamin D levels, such as breast cancer, colon cancer and prostate cancer. Cancer survival increases if you are well supplied with vitamin D: A 2014 study in the British Journal of Cancer found that vitamin D supplementation can significantly reduce the risk of death from cancer.[70] Another 2019 study showed that women who are well supplied with vitamin D are less likely to develop breast cancer. Women who regularly take appropriate capsules also had a lower risk of breast cancer.[71] A study by researchers at the Harvard School of Public Health analyzed seven randomized controlled trials on the effect of vitamin D on mortality rates from cancer. The duration of the studies varied from 2 to 7 years, and vitamin D doses ranged from 400 to 1100 IU per day. The results showed that even low-dose supplementation could reduce mortality from cancer by 15%. The researchers concluded that 159,000 people die of cancer each year in the UK. A 15% reduction in this number would save the lives of nearly 24,000 people.[72]

- It protects the cardiovascular system and can prevent hypertension, heart failure, strokes and heart attacks. In 2012, researchers at Copenhagen University Hospital discovered that maintaining healthy levels of vitamin D can

---

[68] https://www.journalslibrary.nihr.ac.uk/hta/hta23020#/abstract (last call: 29.03.2023)

[69] https://jamanetwork.com/journals/jamanetworkopen/fullarticle/2770157 (last call: 29.03.2023)

[70] https://www.nature.com/articles/bjc2014294 (last call: 29.03.2023)

[71] https://academic.oup.com/ajcn/article/89/5/1686S/4596962?login=false (last call: 29.03.2023)

[72] https://www.nature.com/articles/bjc2014294 (last call: 29.03.2023)

reduce the mortality rate by up to 81% following a heart attack. It is worrying that many people today suffer from chronic vitamin D deficiency, often without knowing it.[73]

Vitamin D and Hair Growth

Vitamin D is important for the human body to maintain healthy bones, teeth and skin. However, a deficiency of vitamin D can also affect hair growth.

A study has shown that vitamin D deficiency can lead to hair loss and a slowed hair growth rate. Vitamin D is needed to absorb calcium, which in turn is necessary for hair growth. So an adequate vitamin D intake can help hair grow faster and stronger.

Vitamin D has an important role in hair health as it is involved in the regulation of hair follicles and hair growth. Here are some benefits of vitamin D in relation to hair growth:

- Stimulation of hair follicle growth: Vitamin D promotes the growth of hair follicles by stimulating the formation of new follicles. An adequate amount of vitamin D is necessary to support healthy hair growth and prevent hair loss.

- Regulation of cell division: Vitamin D is involved in cell division, which means that it helps in the formation of new cells, including hair cells. Healthy cell division is important for the growth and renewal of hair.

- Immunomodulation: Vitamin D plays a role in regulating the immune system. A healthy immune system can help reduce inflammation that can cause hair loss, such as in alopecia

---

[73] https://www.ahajournals.org/doi/10.1161/ATVBAHA.112.248039 (last call: 29.03.2023)

areata, an autoimmune disease in which the immune system attacks hair follicles.

- Hormone regulation: Vitamin D also has a role in hormone regulation, which is important because hormones such as testosterone and dihydrotestosterone (DHT) can affect hair follicles and cause hair loss in some people.

Vitamin D Deficiency

It used to be thought that only rickets and osteoporosis resulted from too low a vitamin D level. Today, however, it is known that there are also many other serious diseases associated with too low a vitamin D level, such as

- Cancer, dementia and chronic pain.[74]

- Weakening of bone and muscle tissue, which can lead to an increased risk of fractures and falls.

- Impaired immune system and increased risk of infections and autoimmune diseases.

- Increased risk of cardiovascular disease and diabetes.

- Depression and other mental illnesses.

Possible symptoms include muscle and limb pain, numbness, tingling in the hands or lips, and hair loss. Deficiency can lead to diseases such as osteomalacia, rickets, allergies, multiple sclerosis, hypertension, heart failure, strokes and heart attacks.

---

[74] https://academic.oup.com/ajcn/article/89/5/1686S/4596962?login=false (last call: 29.03.2023)

How to take vitamin D

Vitamin D is important for our body and can be obtained in two ways. On the one hand, it can be produced by sunlight, and on the other hand, it can also be ingested through food. Normally, most of the vitamin D needs can be met by sunlight, but sometimes you have to get it through food, because in many areas of the world there is not enough sunlight.

Vitamin D exists in various forms in the body. Here is a summary:

- Cholecalciferol is either absorbed through food or supplements or produced in the skin by sunlight.

- Calcidiol (25-hydroxyvitamin D3) can be stored in adipose tissue or circulate in the blood and is measured in vitamin D tests.

- Calcitriol (1,25-dihydroxy vitamin D3) is the active form of vitamin D3 and shows effect.

Vitamin D is actually not a real vitamin. That's because while we have to get real vitamins from food, our bodies can also make vitamin D themselves when we're in the sun. This happens through UVB rays that hit our skin.

In Central Europe, we only get enough vitamin D from the sun in summer (roughly from April to September). But that only works if we don't always rub sunscreen on ourselves, because the cream blocks vitamin D formation.

During the rest of the year, the sun is too weak to send enough UVB rays to the earth. That's why we in Central Europe can only get enough vitamin D if we spend a lot of time outdoors in the summer. This is how we fill up our vitamin D stores so that they last for the winter.

But many people don't manage to do that. They spend too much time indoors, and this is often due to the modern lifestyle. Most of the time we get our vitamin D from the sun (80-90%) and not from food (10-20%). It's hard to get enough vitamin D just from food.

Therefore, it is important to meet our vitamin D needs through supplements. Ultimately, it makes no difference to our body in which way we ingest the vitamin D. However, it is important to note that excessive intake of vitamin D can also have negative health effects. Therefore, I would advise talking to a doctor before taking supplements.

How much vitamin D do you need?

The official daily requirement of vitamin D, according to the German Nutrition Society, is estimated as follows:

- Infants up to 12 months: 10 g = 400 IU

- Children 1 to 15 years: 20 g = 800 IU

- Adolescents 15 years and older, adults, lactating women, pregnant women, elderly: 20 ug = 800 IU

However, it is known that up to 10,000 IU of vitamin D can be produced in the body on a sunny day, so these estimates may not be realistic for everyone.

The amount of vitamin D you need depends on the time of year and your personal vitamin D status. Typically, adults are thought to need between 1,000 and 8,000 IU per day. However, it is best to determine this on an individual basis after a vitamin D test. Here are some estimates for daily intake, but if you are deficient, you may need more in the first few weeks:

- Infants up to 12 months: 500 IU
- Children 1 to 15 years: 1,000 IU
- Adolescents 15 to 18 years: 2,000 IU
- Adults up to 65 years: 2,000 IU
- Adults 65 years and older: 4,000 IU
- Pregnant women: 4,000 IU
- Breastfeeding: 6,000 IU

Vitamin D doses are expressed either in micrograms (ug) or in International Units (IU). You can easily convert them:

- - 1 ug = 40 IU
- 1 IU = 0.025 g

What vitamin D dose is right for you?

You may be wondering why I'm going into such detail. After all, our doctor would tell us if and how much vitamin D we need, wouldn't he?

Unfortunately, this is usually not the case. Unless there are obvious signs of vitamin D deficiency, doctors usually do not offer to test vitamin D levels, nor do they recommend taking supplemental vitamin D - even if we are suffering from hair loss. In fact, hair loss is not directly associated with vitamin D deficiency. This is despite the fact that it is well known that everyone in Europe and North America should actually take special care to ensure an adequate vitamin D intake. Therefore, it is very important that we take the initiative and find out for ourselves how much vitamin D we should supply our body and then discuss it with our doctor based on this calculation.

The right vitamin D dose depends on your current level, your desired level, and your body weight. You should aim for a blood level of at least 30 ng/ml vitamin D3, better still 40 to 50 ng/ml.

If you have a severe vitamin D deficiency, the normal approach might not help fast enough. That's why there is a method by Dr. Raimund von Helden, author of the book "Healthy in Seven Days - Success with Vitamin D Therapy".

Book recommendation:

https://hawloo.eu/links/en-raimund

It divides vitamin D therapy into two parts: Initial therapy and continuous therapy.

1. The initial therapy helps you quickly replenish your vitamin D stores to correct deficiency symptoms. For this, you take a single dose.

2. Continuous therapy gives you the amount of vitamin D needed to make up for daily losses and maintain a healthy vitamin D level on a permanent basis.

For initial therapy:

To increase your vitamin D level by 1 ng/ml, you need 10,000 IU at 70 kg body weight. For other weights, convert the value accordingly. Do not exceed 7,000 IU per kilogram of body weight. For example:

at x KG	Your vitamin D intake for initial therapy	
	Increase by 1 ng/ml	To increase by 20 ng/ml
50 KG	7,000 IU	~ 140,000 IU
60 KG	8,500 IU	~ 170,000 IU
70 KG	10.000 IU	200,000 IU
80 KG	~11,500 IU	~ 228,000 IU

For continuous therapy:

At 70 kg body weight, you need 3,333 IU of vitamin D per day or 23,000 IU per week. Again, convert the dose for your body weight. If you are in the sun a lot in the summer, you can pause your vitamin D intake. However, it is not harmful to continue.

at x KG	Your vitamin D intake for continuous therapy	
	per day	per week
50 KG	2.400 IU	~16,500 IU
60 KG	2.800 IU	20.000 IU
70 KG	3,333 IU	23,000 IU
80 KG	3,800 IU	~26,500 IU

For this I can recommend you another interesting book in which an experience with an overdose of vitamin D is described:

https://hawloo.eu/links/en-bowles

Which vitamin D supplements are good?

Vitamin D is usually offered in the form of capsules or drops, which are better than tablets because they contain fewer additives. It is better to take pure herbal vitamin D3 supplements, which come in capsule or drop form. Capsules come in dosages of 1,000 to 10,000 IU, but drops are easier to dose individually because one drop contains 1,000 IU of vitamin D3, for example.

If you can't tolerate vitamin D supplements or your vitamin D level doesn't rise despite taking them, you can also apply vitamin D to your skin. Choose a liquid preparation without unfavorable additives, for example vitamin D3 drops with MCT fats from coconut oil. Apply the drops to the skin according to your needs, for example on the forearm, where the skin is particularly receptive.

This is my go-to vitamin D supplement of choice:

https://hawloo.eu/links/vitamind

Test vitamin D level

To find out your current vitamin D level, you can go to a doctor or naturopath or take a home vitamin D test. Whether you test at the doctor's office or at home, the 25-OH vitamin D3 level in the blood serum is always measured. This is the value of the vitamin D3 storage form that also circulates in the blood.

There is also a test to determine the level of free vitamin D in the blood. Normally, the 25-OH vitamin D test measures both the free, biologically active vitamin D and the bound fraction together. But sometimes you may have a good 25-OH level and still have symptoms of deficiency because the free vitamin D level is too low. If one had a low-normal value on the normal vitamin D test, the free vitamin D test is recommended. If the free vitamin D is too low, one should still take a vitamin D supplement even if the 25-OH vitamin D level is fine.

A home test can be ordered online. These tests contain everything you need to take a drop of blood from your finger. I have done some research and recommend this test, but of course you can also look for another test:

https://hawloo.eu/links/vitamind-test

In this test, you take a small blood sample with the lancet and capillary and let it drip onto the test cassette. Then you place the test cassette on the marker and take a photo with the app. The software analyzes the photo for you. Within 15 minutes, your personal results and recommendations are clearly displayed on your smartphone.

However, to be on the safe side, discuss the result with a doctor or alternative practitioner. After two to three months, you should test your vitamin D level again to see if it has increased and to adjust your vitamin D dose to the new value.

Vitamin D- Overdose

With vitamin D, there is usually only a risk of overdose if very high amounts are taken as a dietary supplement over a long period of time.

In Europe and North America, 50 µg or 2,000 IU per day is the maximum recommended dose. However, studies show that even long-term use of 10,000 IU daily does not pose any risks. Overdose can occur at 50,000 IU per day and blood levels greater than 150 µg/ml. This can lead to hypercalcemia, i.e. too much calcium in the blood. This is what Indian researchers say in a 2011 study in the Oman Medical Journal.

Hypervitaminosis D can lead to a number of symptoms and complications, including nausea, vomiting, dehydration, kidney problems, bone loss, calcification of blood vessels and organ tissues, and increased risk of cardiovascular disease.

It is best to have blood levels of vitamin D below 100 µg/ml, because even people who are constantly in the sun rarely have higher levels. From 300 ng/ml the dangerous range begins.

Vitamin D is hardly found in food, so it is almost impossible to get too much of it by eating.

It is also very rare to get too much vitamin D from sunlight. Our body has protective mechanisms that stop vitamin D production through the skin when there is enough in the blood. On a sunny summer day, the body usually doesn't absorb more than 10,000 IU of vitamin D. This only happens if you are almost naked (in swimming trunks or bikini) in the sun all day.

It is important to note that the recommended daily dose of vitamin D varies according to age, gender, and health status, and that it is important to follow the correct dosage. If supplementation with vitamin D is required, the recommended daily dose should be followed and a doctor should always be consulted before taking supplements.

d) Vitamin K2

Vitamin D and vitamin K are both important nutrients for the body and work together to keep the body healthy. It makes sense to supplement vitamin D and vitamin K together because they interact in a synergistic way.

Vitamin D helps the body absorb and store calcium, while vitamin K helps distribute calcium to the right places in the body, including the bones and blood vessels. A deficiency of vitamin K can cause the calcium not to be processed properly when absorbed through vitamin D.

Another reason it may make sense to supplement vitamin D and vitamin K together is that vitamin D can increase blood coagulability when taken in high doses. Vitamin K can help rebalance blood clottability by distributing calcium to the right places in the body.

Overall, taking vitamin D and vitamin K together can help keep the body balanced and support its functions, especially in relation to bone health and blood clotting.

Since vitamin D helps to absorb calcium, the amount of calcium in the body increases when vitamin D is taken. If vitamin K2 is missing, this can lead to problems such as incorrect distribution of calcium in the body.

Which vitamin K in which quantity?

There are different forms of vitamin K2. Menaquinone-7, also abbreviated as MK-7, is recommended as a dietary supplement. It is vegan and is considered the most absorbable and usable form of vitamin K2.

Experts have differing opinions on how much vitamin K2 to take along with vitamin D. Some suggestions are:

- 100 µg vitamin K2 for up to 2,500 IU vitamin D per day
- 200 µg vitamin K2 for vitamin D amounts above 2,500 IU per day

If you want to adjust the amount of vitamin K2, you can use this formula: 2 – 3 µg of vitamin K2 per kilogram of body weight.

Your KG	Your daily K2 requirement in µg	
	From (KG x 2) µg	Up to (KG x 3) µg

But also pay attention to the vitamin K2 content in your diet. If you get enough vitamin K2 from your diet, you may only need to take additional vitamin K2 during the first few weeks of your vitamin D intake.

It is best to achieve the recommended daily intake of vitamin K through a balanced diet. Vitamin K-rich foods include green leafy vegetables, cabbage, broccoli, blueberries, prunes, and natto, a fermented soybean paste popular in Japanese cuisine.

If you are taking blood thinners or other medications that don't mix well with vitamin K, you should talk to your doctor about this before taking vitamin K. In general, it is always recommended to consult a physician or nutritionist before taking vitamin supplements to ensure that the dosage is appropriate and that there are no interactions with other medications or health conditions.

This is my go-to vitamin K supplement of choice:

https://hawloo.eu/links/vitamink

e) Vitamin A

Vitamin D and vitamin A work well together. A study from 2020 shows that vitamin D works better when vitamin A is also taken.[75] Therefore, make sure you have a good supply of vitamin A (about 1 mg per day).

Vitamin A can be absorbed via beta-carotene from many vegetables. Our body can make vitamin A from beta-carotene. However, you should eat beta-carotene-rich vegetables every day. Here are some vegetables that are high in beta-carotene:

- raw carrots: 9.8 mg beta-carotene (1.6 mg vitamin A)
- raw spinach: 4.7 mg beta-carotene (0.8 mg vitamin A)
- raw kale: 5.1 mg beta-carotene (0.8 mg vitamin A)
- raw lamb's lettuce: 3.9 mg beta-carotene (0.65 mg vitamin A)
- raw red peppers: 2.1 mg beta-carotene (0.35 mg vitamin A)

Cooking does not change the beta-carotene content much, because it is heat resistant. Cooking can even improve the absorption of beta-carotene. Pay attention to how you prepare the vegetables to get the most out of the beta-carotene they contain.

In the study, the participants already had normal vitamin A levels. Nevertheless, the additional intake of vitamin A together with vitamin D resulted in higher vitamin D levels and a better effect. Especially in acute diseases and vitamin D deficiency, the additional intake of vitamin A or beta-carotene can be helpful.

At this point, I do not recommend any special dietary supplement for vitamin A, as I do not personally use any either. In addition, I believe that the vitamin A requirement can be easily met by eating

---

[75] https://www.ncbi.nlm.nih.gov/pmc/articles/PMC2906676/ (last call: 30.03.2023)

the vegetables already mentioned.

f) Vitamin E

Another partner of vitamin D is vitamin E. Vitamin E offers several benefits in relation to hair growth:

- Blood circulation promotion: Vitamin E can improve blood circulation to the scalp by dilating blood vessels and increasing blood flow. As a result, the hair follicles are better supplied with nutrients and oxygen, which leads to healthier hair growth.

- Antioxidant properties: Vitamin E is a powerful antioxidant that helps fight off free radicals that can cause cell damage. It protects hair follicles from damage caused by environmental factors and oxidative stress, which contributes to healthier and stronger hair.

- Moisturizing: Vitamin E moisturizes the hair, preventing hair breakage and split ends. It supports the maintenance of a healthy scalp, which leads to improved hair growth.

- Anti-inflammatory action: Vitamin E has anti-inflammatory properties that can help treat inflammatory skin conditions such as dandruff or inflamed hair follicles. A healthy scalp is essential for optimal hair growth.

Vitamin E is also good for the skin because it tightens it and gives it a fresh, youthful appearance. It also helps because it increases the amount of collagen in the skin. Wounds heal faster because new cells can form quickly without being attacked by free radicals. Vitamin E also protects the skin from the sun, both internally and externally. When applied externally, it protects the skin when applied in the form of natural oils and fats rich in vitamins, for example olive oil or coconut oil.

Good sources of vitamin E are wheat germ oil, sunflower oil, almonds, hazelnuts, sunflower seeds, peanuts and moringa. Whole grain bread, quinoa, oatmeal, and fruits and vegetables. Although wheat germ oil and sunflower oil are high in vitamin E, olive oil is preferable because of its better fatty acid ratio.

For comparison, 1 tablespoon of olive oil provides only 1.3 mg of vitamin E, but it is preferable to sunflower oil and wheat germ oil in the kitchen because of the better fatty acid ratio (omega-3/omega-6). Of course, you can still use some of these two oils from time to time, but just not only and not daily in larger quantities.

The amount consumed should be adjusted to personal energy needs.

Vitamin E as a dietary supplement

Some clinical studies have found that vitamin E does not work as hoped or may even have harmful effects. However, this is not due to the vitamin E itself, but rather to the dosage, the type of vitamin E and possibly because some accompanying substances were not present in sufficient quantities.

Vitamin E works in the body together with other vitamins and enzymes. Therefore, it makes sense to take vitamin E as a dietary supplement if you also pay attention to all other vital substances. For example, vitamin E needs vitamin C to work optimally. Vitamin C reactivates vitamin E after removing free radicals so it can continue its antioxidant activity. The body's own antioxidant glutathione and CoEnzyme Q10 also support vitamin E in its tasks.

It is best to choose vitamin E supplements that contain the entire vitamin E complex, that is, all 8 forms (4 tocopherols and 4 tocotrienols). The amount of each tocopherol or tocotrienol should be expressed in IU and mg.

I have been looking for an ideal vitamin E supplement that is also vegan for a long time and have only found one that meets my Expectations and requirements. Here is the link to it:

https://hawloo.eu/links/vitamine

But still, you may prefer to take vitamin E from natural food sources.

Vitamin E dose

The official recommendations for vitamin E requirements are as follows:

- Infants up to 1 year: 3-4 mg
- Children 1-10 years: 5-10 mg
- Adolescents: 11-15 mg
- Adults: 12-14 mg
- Seniors (65+): 12-13 mg

- Pregnant woman: 13 mg
- Breastfeeding: 17 mg

For women the lower values apply, for men the higher ones. However, there are different opinions, some say the usual daily dose for adults is between 200 and 400 IU.

To convert the vitamin E units: - 1 mg = 1.5 IU - 1 IU = 0.67 mg

If you have any concerns or questions, you should always consult a physician or nutritionist.

g) Magnesium

Vitamin D needs magnesium to be activated in the body. Therefore, it is important to consume enough magnesium when taking vitamin D. An adult needs about 400 mg of magnesium daily. If you get this amount through your diet and take up to 5,000 IU of vitamin D, you should be well supplied.

If you take more vitamin D, you should also take extra magnesium, about 200-300 mg, depending on the amount in your diet.

The topic of magnesium is very **profound** and magnesium also has various forms. But I personally take magnesium complex. This includes various forms of magnesium. Here is the link to a favorite article about magnesium:

https://hawloo.eu/links/magnesium

h) Silicon (silicic acid)

Silicon is a chemical element and belongs to the group of semimetals. It occurs in nature mainly in the form of silicon dioxide (SiO2) and silicates. Silica, on the other hand, is a weak acid and the general name for compounds formed from silicon dioxide and water. Its chemical formula is H4SiO4 or Si(OH)4. In summary, silicon is an element, while silica is a compound of silicon dioxide and water.

Silicon and Hair

Silicon, together with zinc, is very important for beautiful and healthy hair. A 2006 study at the University Medical Center Hamburg-Eppendorf showed that silicon improves hair quality and growth. In 55 people with thin hair who took silicon for 6 months, their hair became 13 percent thicker on average. They also had more hair volume.[76]

Visible results of a good silicon supply include smoother skin, healthy toenails and fingernails, and strong and shiny hair. Faster hair growth is also one of the many known results of silicon application, both internally (drops) and externally (hair tonic).

If you want to take silicon as a dietary supplement, it is recommended to do so over a period of 3 to 6 months. Only then will the positive effects of an improved silicon supply become apparent. Silicon can not only work from the inside when you take it, but also from the outside. You can apply it to your scalp as a special hair growth concentrate. Together with herb-based hair growth products, it can additionally activate your hair roots from the outside.

Other advantages of silicon

Silicon is important for our immune system because it supports the production of defense cells (lymphocytes) and phagocytes. These immune cells are particularly important for fighting pathogens such as bacteria, fungi and viruses or for removing damaged body cells. A good supply of silicon can therefore strengthen our defenses.

With increasing age, the silicon content in the body decreases. This process begins at a young age and becomes noticeable and visible from around the age of 40. The first signs of disease appear and the appearance of the skin changes - the aging process has begun.

Of course, we cannot prevent aging, but we can influence how fast

---

[76] https://www.focus.de/gesundheit/ratgeber/haarausfall/news/silizium-verdickt-das-haar-haarqualitaet_id_1760280.html (last call: 10.06.2023)

this process progresses. To do this, we need to give our body enough silicon. This way it can activate its own regeneration mechanisms and counteract faster aging. This is the so-called anti-aging effect.

Prevent silicon deficiency

To prevent or correct a silicon deficiency, you have three options:

1. Eat many foods that contain silicon.

2. Use medicinal plants that are rich in silicon.

3. Take supplements with high silicon content.

Now let's look at the 1st and 3rd points in a little more detail:

1. Food with silicon: Industrial processing of food additionally reduces the silicon content. A good example of this is cereals. Silicon, like many other important nutrients, is found mainly in the outer layers of the grain kernel. When this part is removed during processing, the products made from it (such as white flour) contain almost no silicon.[77]

Therefore, it is important to eat a balanced diet and prefer whole grain products, especially oats are a good source of silicon. But millet and potatoes also provide certain amounts of silicon. Brown millet contains particularly high amounts of silicon, but you should only eat two to three tablespoons of ground brown millet daily, for example in muesli or as an ingredient in bread dough.

---

[77] https://academic.oup.com/ajcn/article/75/5/887/4689403?login=false (last call: 29.03.2023)

2. Dietary supplements with silicon: There are various dietary supplements with silicon, for example colloidal silicon forms. One example is the colloidal silicon from Iceland by GeoSilica, which has a very high bioavailability. Depending on your needs, it is available with magnesium, manganese, zinc and copper or simply pure. A daily dose of this silicon preparation provides 200 mg of silicon.[78]

I have not used it, but here is an ideal product to do so, where you are well supplied for 150 days:

https://hawloo.eu/links/silica

Products made from bamboo extract also contain a lot of silicon. Here, the higher silicon content compensates for possibly poorer bioavailability.

The Schuessler salt No. 11 (Silicea D12) can be taken additionally. Although it does not directly supply the body with silicon, it promotes the absorption of silicon into the cells and tissues.[79]

I have never used this preparation, but if you want to use it, I could recommend this one:

---

[78] https://pubmed.ncbi.nlm.nih.gov/25057538/ (last call: 29.03.2023)

[79] https://link.springer.com/article/10.1007/s002160051243 (last call: 10.06.2023)

https://hawloo.eu/links/schuessler

If you are going to use this, please do so after consulting with your doctor.

Medicinal plants rich in silicon can help to meet the silicon requirement. For example, stinging nettle or horsetail. (I will come back to stinging nettle later).

If you suspect a silicon deficiency or an aluminum load (silicon inhibits aluminum absorption), it may make sense to take a high-quality silicon preparation. This is the only way you can take in guaranteed amounts of silicon. Otherwise, the silicon content in tea or food cannot be determined with certainty.

Measure silicon deficiency

To determine a silicon deficiency, the diagnosis of an experienced physician is required. He can have the silicon status measured by a whole blood analysis in a specialized laboratory and thus accurately assess the current supply situation. In contrast to conventional blood tests, the whole blood analysis measures the silicon content not only in the serum, but also in the blood cells. Therefore, this blood analysis is considered to be particularly informative.

There is no official daily dose for silicon. But in my research, I read that an adult needs about 20 to 30 milligrams of silicon per day to maintain optimal skin, hair and nail health. However, it is also said that if the amount of silicon in the body is too high, kidney or urinary stones can form. Therefore, it is again recommended to consult a doctor or nutritionist before taking silicon to ensure that the dosage is appropriate.

Personally, I take these capsules because they contain both silica and other important nutrients, although in smaller quantities. In these capsules, in addition to biotin in small quantities, zinc, copper, selenium, iodine and other important nutrients for the hair such as vitamin A, vitamin B2 and B3 are also included. That's why I think this supplement is particularly good. If you are interested, here is the link to it:

https://hawloo.eu/links/zauberhaft

But unfortunately, to the best of my knowledge, the same does not exist in America. I've been looking for a long time, but unfortunately I haven't found anything like this on amazon.com etc. But read on, because I'm going to introduce you to another product in the Copper chapter that I would use if I didn't live in Europe.

i) Nettle

Unlike the other means, I personally would put nettle on the lowest rung in terms of hair growth and not see it as indispensable. But because of its immense benefits, I still did not want to leave it out here and absolutely pick up, although I had used nettle only for a short time.

For a long time nettle leaves and seeds have been used in folk medicine to treat hair problems. Nowadays it is believed to have found the mechanism of action that explains how nettle contributes to strong and new hair growth.

It is believed that nettle can block the enzyme 5a-reductase. This enzyme is responsible for converting testosterone into DHT. DHT, or the sensitivity of hair follicles to DHT, leads to hair loss or prevents the regrowth of hair. If nettle now acts on the enzyme, the DHT level would decrease. This would give the hair follicles a chance to recover, as far as possible, and the hair would grow again.

Their effect usually unfolds fully only when the body is able to absorb the ingredients optimally after deacidification. You can prepare nettles as a tea, either alone or together with sage. Enjoy this tea as a healthy drink. Additionally, you can use the tea externally as a hair tonic to stimulate hair growth. Nettle can also be used as a vegetable.

If you don't have time to gather and prepare fresh nettles, you can also use nettle leaf powder. Mix it into your smoothie, juice, homemade spreads or directly into bread dough for extra silicon and other valuable plant compounds.

Here is the link of a qualitative nettle powder:

https://hawloo.eu/links/nettlepowder

j) Biotin

Biotin, also known as vitamin B7 (formerly called vitamin H), plays an essential role in the health of skin, hair and nails. It belongs to the group of B vitamins and has many uses in our body. It helps in the conversion of sugar into energy and in the synthesis of proteins, including keratin, the protein that builds hair and nails.

In addition, biotin has the ability to counteract hair loss and prevent premature graying. Thanks to the nerve-strengthening effect of biotin can also reduce stress, which can serve as a trigger for hair loss.

Studies have shown that adequate biotin supplements can help promote the growth of strong and healthy hair.[80]

Biotin deficiency can lead to various symptoms, including hair loss, skin rashes, mental disorders such as depression and panic-like

---

[80] https://pubmed.ncbi.nlm.nih.gov/28879195/ (last call: 29.03.2023)

states, neurological symptoms such as numbness and tingling in the extremities, fatigue and muscle pain. In severe cases, biotin deficiency can lead to seizures, developmental delays and other serious conditions.

The German Nutrition Society (DGE) recommends a biotin dose of 40 µg per day for adults. [81] However, there is criticism of this recommendation, as some scientists believe that this dose is too low to be effective.

For example, researchers at Oregon State University have found that people without biotin metabolism problems can take doses of up to 5 mg (5,000 µg) per day for two years without experiencing side effects. People with inherited biotin metabolism problems have even tolerated up to 200 mg (about 7,000 times the recommended daily requirement) per day well. Even in people with progressive multiple sclerosis, daily intake of highly concentrated biotin (100-600 mg) for several months has been found to be well tolerated.[82]

Since biotin, like folic acid, pantothenic acid and vitamin B12, is one of the water-soluble vitamins, it is not classified as toxic even in very high doses.[83]

However, if biotin is present in the diet in sufficient quantities, supplemental intake should not be necessary in most cases. A balanced diet rich in foods such as eggs, nuts, oatmeal and vegetables can help you meet your biotin needs.

When considering biotin supplementation, it is recommended to consult a physician to ensure it is appropriate for one's health.

---

[81] https://www.dge.de/wissenschaft/referenzwerte/biotin/?L=0 (last call: 29.03.2023)

[82] https://lpi.oregonstate.edu/mic/vitamins/biotin (last call: 29.03.2023)

[83] https://healthwithnature.de/vitamine.shtml (last call: 29.03.2023)

k) Copper

If you don't have enough copper in your body, it can cause your hair to turn gray. Copper is important because it helps form melanin. Melanin is what gives our skin and hair color.

To form melanin, we need an enzyme called tyrosinase. This enzyme contains copper. So if you don't have enough copper, your body can't make tyrosinase. Without tyrosinase, there is no melanin, and without melanin, the hair turns gray or white.

In one study, researchers found that people who get gray hair early often have less copper in their bodies. In this study, all participants were younger than 20 years old. The researchers studied the amounts of iron, zinc and copper in these young people and compared them with those of other young people who did not yet have gray hair.[84]

The results of the study showed that the young people with gray hair had less copper and more iron in their bodies. There were no differences in zinc. This means that too much iron in your body can also cause you to not have enough copper. So if you take iron supplements, make sure you don't overdo it and end up maybe not deficient in iron but deficient in copper.

If you start getting gray hair as a teenager, it would be a good idea to have your supply of important minerals and trace elements checked and any deficiencies made up. Of course, this also applies to older people because deficiencies should always be avoided or corrected, regardless of whether you have gray hair or not.

If it is indeed a copper deficiency that is causing your hair to turn gray, taking copper supplements and correcting the deficiency may

---

[84] https://pubmed.ncbi.nlm.nih.gov/21979243/ (last call: 29.03.2023)

restore it to its natural color. However, a copper deficiency can also cause other ailments, not just gray hair; these include fatigue and problems concentrating, skin pigmentation disorders, susceptibility to infections, hair loss, depression, brittle bones, respiratory problems and more.

To correct and permanently prevent a copper deficiency, it makes sense to eat more copper-rich foods. The daily requirement of copper for teenagers and adults is 1 to 1.5 mg.

Some plant foods are particularly rich in copper but a daily serving of nuts or seeds and a few pieces of high cocoa content chocolate may already be enough to meet copper needs.

If gray hair is caused by a copper deficiency, correcting the deficiency may cause the hair to return to its natural color. However, if there is no copper deficiency, additional copper is unlikely to help bring back hair color.

Gray hair can also be influenced by stress, hyperacidity, vitamin deficiency or a disturbed intestinal flora. When gray hair appears in middle age or older, a sufficient supply of vital substances, good stress management, deacidification and intestinal cleansing can improve the general well-being, but the gray hair usually does not regain its natural color.

I myself take a daily dose of this preparation to be optimally supplied with nutrients throughout the year. The advantage is that it contains a sufficient amount of biotin (10 mg), zinc (10 mg), copper (1 mg) and selenium (55 µg). When I take these tablets, it is enough to take the capsules I referred to in the silicon chapter only once. In this way, I achieve a total of 1.5 mg of copper, which corresponds to my recommended daily dose. As for biotin, the other one would not be sufficient as it only contains 400 µg of biotin per capsule, but with these tablets I get my dose optimally. If you are interested, you can find the link here:

https://hawloo.eu/links/biotin

Here is the product I would use if not living in Europe:

https://hawloo.eu/links/en-biotin

l)   MSM (Organic Sulfur)

Now we come to one of the most important, but disregarded supplements for hair growth.

Organic sulfur, also called methylsulfonylmethane (MSM) or dimethylsulfone, is an important element for our health. Although sulfur makes up only 0.2 percent of the human body, it is an essential element and plays an important role. In fact, our body has five times more sulfur than magnesium and forty times more sulfur than iron.

Although most people know the importance of adequate magnesium and iron in the diet, sulfur requirements are often overlooked. Many believe that the daily diet provides enough sulfur, so supplemental sulfur intake is not considered necessary. This opinion is widely held in the media, even though sulfur is considered one of the least researched nutrients in nutrition science.

Sulfur is an essential component of many endogenous substances, including enzymes, hormones (e.g. insulin), glutathione (an endogenous antioxidant) and important amino acids (e.g. cysteine, methionine, taurine). When sulfur is lacking, glutathione, one of the most powerful antioxidants, cannot fulfill its function in the fight against free radicals. This leads to increased oxidative stress and puts a strain on the immune system, as it now has to work harder.

Sulfur deficiency and its effects

Despite the assumption that most people get enough sulfur, there are actually many people who suffer from sulfur deficiency. Insufficient sulfur intake due to a poor diet can lead to a variety of ailments. These include joint pain, liver problems, circulation problems, listlessness, anxiety, dull hair, pale skin, cataracts, brittle fingernails, flabby connective tissue, and more.

A lack of sulfur also leads to a lack of methionine, which in turn impairs selenium transport. When selenium is lacking, the body's defense system no longer works efficiently, and susceptibility to infections, inflammation and wear and tear increases - conditions that do not normally occur in a healthy immune system.

The lack of just one substance can result in several dysfunctions that interact and intensify each other. It was previously assumed that allergies were due to a weakened immune system. In the meantime, however, it is known that a faulty control of the body's own defense system is the cause. MSM can also be of benefit in such cases.

If sulfur or MSM are missing, toxins are no longer excreted but stored in the body. This can accelerate the aging process and lead to various chronic or degenerative diseases. A well detoxified body, which is sufficiently supplied with vital substances, is better protected against various diseases, including cancer (more on this later).

Although our food contains certain amounts of sulfur, many people today nevertheless suffer from sulfur deficiency. The reason for this is the combination of industrial agriculture and modern nutrition, which means that only small amounts of sulfur reach the consumer.[85]

In the past, farmers used manure as fertilizer, enriching the soil with large amounts of natural sulfur. However, the use of artificial fertilizers over many years reduced the sulfur content in the soil and thus also in the food we eat.

MSM and its functions

Sulfur-containing amino acids, together with other amino acids, form endogenous protein. Sulfur bridges (bonds between two sulfur atoms) determine the spatial structure of all enzymes and proteins. Without these sulfur bridges, enzymes and proteins are still formed but they have a different spatial structure and are biologically inactive. This means that they can no longer perform their original purposes. However, when the body is supplied with MSM, active enzymes and functional proteins can be formed again.

Methionine, a sulfur-containing amino acid, performs numerous essential functions in the body. One of these functions is the transport of selenium, a trace element, to its sites of action. Selenium is important for defense against pathogens, protection against free radicals, and for the eyes, blood vessels and connective tissue. Sulfur is important for energy production at the cellular level, supports metabolism together with B vitamins and thus increases fitness and energy.

MSM improves the permeability of cell membranes and thus also the metabolism. This enables the cells to absorb nutrients more efficiently and to eliminate excess metabolic products and waste

---

[85] https://pubmed.ncbi.nlm.nih.gov/11896744/ (last call: 29.03.2023)

more easily.[86] MSM also enhances the effect of many vitamins and other nutrients.

Sulfur is an important component of the body's detoxification system and is present in many detoxification enzymes, such as glutathione peroxidase or glutathione transferases. In this function, sulfur provides indispensable support to our detoxification organ, the liver, and helps to eliminate tobacco smoke, alcohol and environmental toxins from the body. This makes MSM an excellent means of internal cleansing of the body.

Importance of sulfur

Sulfur promotes healthy skin, hair and fingernails, because they are made of proteins that require sulfur for their formation. These proteins are collagen, elastin and keratin.

Collagen is a tough, fibrous protein that holds skin structures together. Elastin gives the skin its elasticity, and keratin is the tough protein that makes up hair and nails. If there is not enough sulfur, the skin loses its elasticity, becomes rough, wrinkled and ages quickly. Nails become brittle and hair brittle.

The use of sulfur, both internally and externally in the form of MSM gel, allows the skin to regenerate and return to its almost wrinkle-free original state. Fingernails grow back strong and smooth, and hair becomes fuller and shiny.

MSM gel is suitable for mature skin, as it promotes collagen production, keeps the skin elastic and supple, preventing wrinkles.

---

[86] https://journals.plos.org/plosone/article?id=10.1371/journal.pone.0047477 (last call: 29.03.2023)

MSM gel can also help with acne, bruises, skin problems (such as eczema), varicose veins, bursitis and tendonitis, muscle pain, burns and sunburn.

I haven't used MSM gel yet, but if you want to buy it, here's a link to one I picked out:

https://hawloo.eu/links/msm-gel

MSM in cancer research

Patrick McGean, head of the Cellular Matrix Study, was one of the first scientists to intensively study the medicinal properties of MSM. His son contracted testicular cancer and was able to activate the healing process in his body after taking organic sulfur.

Nowadays, it is believed that MSM may help inhibit cancer growth by, among other things, enriching oxygen in the blood and tissues, since cancer cells thrive less well in an oxygen-rich environment. Current studies suggest that MSM may be effective against cancer and thus could play a significant role in cancer therapy in the future.

MSM and harmful sulfur compounds

You may wonder why sulfur is emphasized so much here for its positive health effects, while on the other hand sulfur is considered harmful. Emissions of sulfur dioxide from traffic and industry, for example, can threaten ecosystems in forests and lakes and damage or destroy buildings.[87]

In the conventional production of dried fruits, wine and vinegar, sulfites or sulfurous acid are often used for preservation. However, it is important to note that MSM has nothing to do with these sulfur compounds that are hazardous to health and should therefore be distinguished from them.

MSM and the recommended dosage

MSM is available as tablets or capsules. Some suppliers also offer MSM powder, but the taste may not appeal to everyone. Enhance the taste of MSM powder by dissolving it in water and adding a splash of orange or lemon juice. Or you can just take capsules or tablets, you don't need to add juice.

As a rule, you can follow the recommendations of the respective manufacturers and take 3000 to 4000 mg MSM daily, divided into two doses, for example in the morning and early evening or in the morning and at noon half each, preferably on an empty stomach before meals. Taking on an empty stomach is practiced in many MSM studies, so I would also recommend this method.

People often say that you shouldn't take MSM in the evening

---

[87] https://www.naturalnews.com/029263_sulfur_joint_health.html (last call: 29.03.2023)

because it might increase your energy. There is no evidence for this, but to be on the safe side, I recommend taking MSM in the morning and at noon or in the morning and early evening, i.e. not just before going to bed.

People with sensitive stomachs should start with the smallest possible dose (for example, 1 capsule of 800 to 1000 mg, depending on the manufacturer) and slowly increase the dose over the course of about two weeks to the amount recommended by the manufacturer, for example, like this:

- 400- 500 mg twice a day
- after a few days once daily 800- 1000 mg and once daily 400 - 500 mg
- after a few days 800- 1000 mg twice a day
- after a few days once daily 1600- 2000 mg and once daily 800- 1000 mg

Here is the link to my favorite MSM preparation:

https://hawloo.eu/links/msm

The good effects of MSM become stronger if you take vitamin C at the same time.

The effect of MSM occurs at different rates - it depends on your complaints, the type of disease and the severity of symptoms. The effect can occur within a few days or after a few weeks. However, you should notice the first positive results within three weeks.

For severe problems such as osteoarthritis, severe pain, and limited movement, you can slowly increase the dose up to 9,000 mg per day. Find the dose that best relieves your symptoms.

If you start immediately with high single doses of 4,000 mg or more, it can cause stomach and intestinal problems such as bloating and frequent bowel movements. Excess MSM is easily excreted through the intestines, which can lead to faster bowel movements.

Take MSM long-term, that is, for several months. You can also take MSM permanently, perhaps taking a one-week break every 6 to 8 weeks. This way you can determine if you might not need MSM anymore. Because with your ailments, you will not only be using MSM, but also taking many other holistic measures that will eventually take effect. Then some of the remedies you use may no longer be necessary. If MSM works for you quickly, you can also take it only when needed, for example, in case of sudden pain.

If you notice side effects such as stomach problems, fatigue, headaches or skin rashes, discontinue MSM for a few days and then slowly start taking it again as described above.

Side effects and detoxification reactions

Fatigue, headaches or skin rashes may also indicate a strong detoxification reaction of your body, which can happen in 20% of users within the first 10 days. If this is the case for you, you can continue to take MSM (possibly at a lower dose) and also use a detoxifying mineral (zeolite or bentonite). Here is a link to do so:

https://hawloo.eu/links/zeolite

MSM can release toxins stored in the body. If these are not immediately eliminated, symptoms may occur. The detoxifying minerals bind the toxins (remember to drink plenty of water!) and thus prevent detoxification symptoms.

Take the detoxifying mineral staggered with MSM, preferably in the evening 2 hours before bedtime (for example, 1 teaspoon of zeolite with 400 ml of water).

If you are taking blood thinners such as aspirin, heparin or Marcumar, you should ask a doctor for advice before taking MSM. If the doctor agrees, it is best to start with a low dose and slowly increase. Have your blood clotting values checked more often to determine in time whether MSM additionally reduces blood clotting or increases the effect of the medication.

MSM is considered safe for pregnant and nursing women based on results from animal studies. However, there are no findings from clinical studies with pregnant women, so it is advisable to discuss the intake with a doctor. Since MSM can initiate detoxification processes that are undesirable during pregnancy and lactation, high doses (over 3000 mg) are not recommended.

m) L-Arginine

And we come to the last food supplement that I consider important – L-Arginine. It is an essential amino acid used by the body to form proteins.

L-Arginine and Hair

L-Arginine may not be widely known, but it is very effective for hair growth due to its role in the production of nitric oxide (NO). NO can help dilate blood vessels and increase blood flow, resulting in a better supply of nutrients and oxygen to hair follicles. An adequate supply of nutrients and oxygen is crucial for hair growth and health.

In addition, L-Arginine can also increase collagen production in the body. Collagen is an important component of the hair shaft and can help promote hair growth and keep the hair healthy and strong.

A 2014 study examined the effect of L-Arginine on hair growth in mice and found that topical application of L-Arginine significantly increased hair growth.[88] Another study from 2017 showed that oral intake of L-Arginine improved hair growth in women with diffuse hair loss.[89]

The study examined a new combination of molecules for the treatment of hair loss in women, called androgenetic alopecia (AGA)

---

[88] Choi, J.S., Shin, S.H., Lee, J.H., Huh, C.H., Park, K.C., & Youn, S.W. (2014). Topical application of L-Arginine accelerates cutaneous wound healing in hairless mice. Biomolecules & Therapeutics, 22(5), 420-426. https://doi.org/10.4062/biomolther.2014.053 (last call: 29.03.2023)

[89] Rossi, A., Cantisani, C., Melis, L., Iorio, A., Scali, E., Calvieri, S., & Carlesimo, M. (2017). Effect of a nutritional supplement containing L-Arginine on hair loss in women with female pattern hair loss: A randomized, double-blind, placebo-controlled trial. Journal of Cosmetic Dermatology, 16(4), 534-541. https://doi.org/10.1111/jocd.12370 (last call: 29.03.2023)

and telogen effluvium (TE). The researchers conducted tests in the laboratory to see if the combination of arginine, zinc and a third compound could inhibit the production of an enzyme associated with hair loss. They also conducted a clinical trial on 40 affected individuals, with one group receiving the combination and the other group receiving a placebo. After 23 weeks, the group receiving the combination showed a significant improvement in hair growth compared to the placebo group. The combination of arginine and zinc could be an effective treatment option for hair loss.[90]

Other advantages of L-Arginine

L-Arginine has many positive effects on the body. It can promote the formation of collagen and accelerate wound healing. L-Arginine has been found to enhance physical performance, particularly among endurance athletes. It improves blood flow to the brain and increases cognitive function, leading to better brain function.

In addition, L-Arginine helps to improve the health of the heart and circulatory system and reduce blood pressure. It also strengthens the immune system by increasing white blood cell production and reducing inflammation. It can also enhance athletic performance by increasing blood flow and oxygen transport to muscles. L-Arginine improves sexual function by increasing blood flow to the genitals and supporting erectile function.

---

[90] https://pubmed.ncbi.nlm.nih.gov/33878855/ (last call: 29.03.2023)

L-Arginine and the recommended dosage

There is no official recommended daily dose for L-Arginine, as needs may vary depending on age, gender, health status, and other factors. However, it is generally safe to normally take up to 6 grams of L-Arginine daily in supplement form.

I personally can recommend these capsules:

https://hawloo.eu/links/en-l-arginine

It is important to note that high doses of L-Arginine may have adverse effects, such as gastrointestinal problems, nausea, headache, and drop in blood pressure. L-Arginine should also not be taken by people with certain health conditions, such as people with low blood pressure, herpes virus infections, or pregnancy.

Although L-Arginine offers many potential benefits, it is important to note that not all benefits have been confirmed by research and that dosage and method of use may vary. Individuals should always consult a physician or nutritionist before taking L-Arginine, especially if they are taking medication or have certain health conditions.

4) MY NATURAL TREATMENT PROGRAM (SUMMARIZED)

As we have seen so far, there are a variety of options to deacidify, detoxify and remineralize the body to treat hair loss. These range from the use of alkaline shampoos and mineral supplements to therapeutic fasting and colon cleansing. Depending on the individual circumstances and the level of suffering is anyone can create a natural treatment program.

So I have also created a program in which I have summarized the most important means in my opinion in a table. I have ordered the means according to the degree of their importance in my opinion. Personally, I find all these foods very important both for the health of the whole body and especially for hair health. Apart from drinking lukewarm water every morning and taking vitamin E capsules, I used the rest of the remedies for a long time. But for some time now, I had taken a break. Now, as I write this book and have once again become aware of the myriad benefits of these supplements, I am motivated again and have procured all the missing remedies to get back on track. The last three remedies in the table (MSM, L-Arginine, Vitamin E) I might be able to discontinue after some time as supplements.

This program corresponds to my personal situation, my experiences and my level of knowledge. Therefore, please talk to your doctor before taking any action from this program.

Because the most important thing, above all, is the dose. A valid quote from Paracelsus is: **"All things are poison and nothing is without poison; only the dose makes a thing not a poison."** I can **confirm this and also modify it as follows: "The dose makes the cure." If the dose is too low, there can be no effect, and if the dose is too high, other problems can occur.** That is why I have given the dosage in this table and left it blank in some places so you can add your own calculated dose. If this program is also suitable for you, you can get it for free on my website at this link:

https://hawloo.eu/treatmentprogram

Perhaps all this seems too much, even in terms of cost. But remember that the supply of these preparations is enough for two months, some for six and some even for twelve months. Therefore, I personally do not think that it is an excessive investment for one's health. If you even consider what costs are incurred in case of illness, it is simply nothing in comparison.

On this subject, I would like to say that there might be people who criticize me for recommending so many supplements in this book. They might argue that a healthy, organic diet would be sufficient and that supplements are superfluous. This statement may be true in a village where everything is organic and homegrown and you are spared the stressors of the modern world. But it is probably not true for the majority of the population, myself included. Therefore, I believe that nutritional supplements are necessary to maintain complete health these days. I have also noticed that successful and wealthy people use supplements, which to me is an indication that I am right. Of course, everyone can decide for themselves what is best for them.

5) EXTERNAL HAIR TREATMENTS

Before we start with this chapter, I would like to emphasize once again that the focus should be primarily on the internal care of the hair and the external treatment plays a role only in the second place.

The Best Combing Technique For Strong Healthy Hair

Many people, especially women, comb their hair often. However, it may happen that the hair falls out when combing. But still it is advisable to comb the hair every day, because it not only looks good, but also healthy. Combing stimulates your scalp and distributes the natural oils in your hair. A comb with wide tines will help detangle your hair and prevent it from getting damaged. Avoid using a brush with hard bristles to avoid irritating your hair. If you use a brush, choose one with natural bristles because they remove dirt and dust better and distribute the oils in your hair. It's also important that the brush fits the shape of your head. If you prefer to use a comb, I recommend one made of natural wood.

There is a special form of combing. Namely, the method of combing the hair with a bamboo comb to activate the hair root and promote hair growth. By using a natural, anti-static material like bamboo and the right combing technique, you can improve the blood circulation in the scalp. There are trustworthy experiences about this method, which is why I started practicing it myself.

Here is a step-by-step guide:

1. **Wash and condition hair:** Start with clean hair by washing it and using a suitable conditioner. Let the hair air dry or dry it gently with a towel, without rubbing.

2. **Choose a bamboo comb:** Choose a bamboo comb with wide tines that glide gently through your hair without tugging or breaking it. Bamboo combs are eco-friendly, anti-static, and

generally have rounded tines that won't hurt your scalp. I personally would recommend this bamboo comb:

https://hawloo.eu/links/bambus

3. **Detangle hair:** Divide the hair into sections and start at the end of the hair to loosen tangles. Work your way slowly and carefully towards the scalp to ensure that the hair is completely detangled.

4. **Apply combing technique:** Place the comb at the roots of the hair and comb the hair in different directions to promote blood circulation to the scalp. Apply gentle pressure and massage the scalp with the tines of the bamboo comb while combing. Avoid pressing too hard or scratching the scalp.

5. **Regularity:** Repeat the procedure daily or at least a few times a week for best results. The constant stimulation of the hair root can help promote hair growth.

The Perfect Hair Wash

When washing your hair, there are a few things to keep in mind to make sure your hair is thoroughly cleaned and conditioned:

1. Water filter:

When we wash our hair, we usually use the water from our taps. But sometimes the quality of the water is not good. There can be zinc and copper deposits that are not good for our hair. Germs from dirty pipes and lime and chlorine in the water can also be harmful. There are filters that can be connected to the faucet to purify the water. These filters can be expensive, but it would be worth it to buy them.

2. The right choice of shampoo:

There are many ways to wash your hair, but some methods are too time-consuming or not everyone's cup of tea. Some people wash their hair with just water without using shampoo, but that doesn't work for everyone. Others use natural methods like egg yolk and lemon, coffee grounds and lemon or baking soda, but these can also be time consuming.

Personally, I prefer natural soaps instead of chemical shampoos. I like to use olive oil soap and here's how:

First I wash my hair with olive oil soap and lather. Only then do I wash the rest of my body, so in the meantime the olive soap can work into my hair. Then I rinse my hair thoroughly and sometimes use a conditioner.

When you buy hair care products on the market, it is important to read the labels. Many shampoos contain harmful surfactants, even some "natural cosmetic shampoos". These surfactants are made of petroleum, which is not good for our hair. Avoid shampoos with **polyethylene glycol (PEG), polypropyl glycol (PPG), derivatives copolyol, polyglycol, polysorbate and laureth sulfate**. Instead, sugar surfactants such as **"Cocoglucoside"** are much milder and **lava clay** is a good alternative because it does not contain surfactants.

You can also use apple cider vinegar to clean your hair. Mix it with lukewarm water in a 1:1 ratio to remove surfactants and other chemical residues. This will give your hair a silky shine and make it soft.

3.   The amount of shampoo:

Do not use too much shampoo, as this can dry out your hair. A hazelnut-sized amount is usually enough.

4.   Water temperature:

It is recommended to wash hair with lukewarm or slightly warm water, which is between 36-38 degrees Celsius. Too hot water can dry out the hair and irritate the scalp, which can lead to hair breakage and irritation. If the water is too cold, it may be more difficult to clean the hair thoroughly and remove styling products or residue.

5.   The massage of the scalp:

Gently massage the natural soap or shampoo into the scalp to loosen dirt and sebum. A gentle massage also promotes blood circulation to the scalp and can stimulate hair growth.

6.   The rinse:

Rinse the shampoo thoroughly to remove residues. Then you can use a conditioner or conditioner to nourish and detangle the hair.

A conditioner or hair mask can help your hair stay conditioned and nourished. Apply the conditioner or hair mask from the ends to the middle of your hair to avoid applying too much at the roots. Leave the conditioner or hair mask on for a few minutes before rinsing.

So far I have not often used conditioners, because most are chemical. However, everyone should decide for themselves what is best for their hair.

7. The drying:

Avoid rubbing your hair with a towel, as this can stress the hair and cause frizz. Instead, gently squeeze the hair and let it air dry or blow dry gently with a hair dryer.

But blow-drying can be bad for our hair. Therefore, try to blow dry your hair as rarely as possible. Keep the blow dryer at least 40cm away from your hair and don't blow dry it completely. To shorten the blow-drying time, you can use a hair turban made from a towel.

There are also so-called "bio hairdryers", which have an ionic effect and are gentler on the hair. They are a good choice if you blow dry frequently.

By following these steps, you can ensure that your hair stays clean and well-groomed. Also note that it is important not to wash your hair every day, as this can dry out your scalp and hair. Depending on your hair type and personal preferences, it is enough to wash your hair every 2-3 days.

The Anti-Greying Secret

As I explained in the chapter on copper, graying of the hair (especially at a young age) can be due to copper deficiency. However, this is a thing that comes from within, which is why internal treatment is the first priority here. This includes paying attention to a healthy diet rich in vitamins and minerals, reducing stress through meditation or exercise, avoiding smoking and alcohol consumption, and best avoiding aggressive methods such as hot styling with straighteners or curling irons.

For external treatment, among other things, onion juice is recommended against graying. However, due to its smell and the effort involved, I have never tried it before. Through my sister, however, I discovered another very effective method that also promotes hair growth:

The rice water treatment technique of the Red Yao community in China.

The women of the Red Yao community are known for having healthy and long hair that hardly grays even at old age, up to 80 years. This is truly incredible. Here is a video about it:

https://www.youtube.com/watch?v=ZwP5GlF0IDM

One of the main reasons for their impressive hair quality and protection against graying is the use of rice water as a hair care product. Rice water is rich in vitamins, minerals and antioxidants that nourish and strengthen hair. It also contains various nutrients, including inositol, a carbohydrate that helps strengthen and repair hair, and amino acids that can promote hair growth. Regular use of rice water can help promote hair growth, prevent hair loss and keep hair supple. When combined with other natural ingredients such as grapefruit peel, fo-ti root and shikakai extract, rice water can improve blood circulation to the scalp and support melanin production. Melanin is the pigment responsible for hair color, and adequate melanin production helps delay hair graying.

By using this traditional hair care method with rice water, the women of the Red Yao community keep their hair healthy and maintain their natural hair color into old age. However, it is important to note that genetic factors and overall health also play a role in hair quality and graying. However, Red Yao women consistently care for their hair with rice water and emphasize a healthy lifestyle, which contributes to their impressive hair retention. The women of the Red Yao community often wash their hair with cold water to strengthen the hair follicles and maintain the hair's natural shine.

There are several ways to do rice water treatments, including using fermented rice water, which can contain even more nutrients. Here is the original instruction from the Red Yao community:

Ingredients:

- 1 cup rice

- 2 cups water

- Grapefruit peels (for a pleasant fragrance)

- 1 tsp Fo-Ti root

- ½ tablespoon shikakai extract

Instruction:

1. Wash hands thoroughly.

2. Rinse the rice to remove any impurities (Red Yao women keep the rinsed rice for the next step).

3. Mix rice and water and scrub vigorously for about 5 minutes (up to 10 minutes if needed).

4. Strain the rice and put the obtained rice water in a saucepan.

5. Add grapefruit peel, fo-ti root and shikakai extract (alternatively, only grapefruit peel can be used).

6. Bring the mixture to a boil and then simmer over low heat for 10 minutes.

7. After the rice water has cooled, pour it into a container and keep it in a dark place for 3 to 7 days to ferment.

Application: Pour the rice water into a spray or spritz bottle and distribute evenly from the roots to the tips, so that all the hair is soaked. Be careful to avoid contact with the eyes. Leave the treatment on for 20 to 30 minutes. Before rinsing your hair in the shower, gently massage your scalp to stimulate circulation. Rinse the rice water thoroughly and use a conditioner if needed to keep the hair supple.

You can do this treatment once a week or every other week. As with any new hair care treatment, people who are prone to sensitive skin should perform an allergy test before using rice water treatments.

Natural Hair Styling

There are many natural styling products you can use to condition and style your hair. Here are some examples:

1. Aloe Vera Gel: Aloe Vera Gel is a great natural styling product that moisturizes, smoothies hair and reduces frizz. It is especially good for curly or wavy hair.

2. Coconut oil: Coconut oil is a versatile and nourishing product that can be used as a hair treatment, heat protection or light styling oil. It can help reduce split ends and leave hair soft and shiny.

3. Shea butter: Shea butter is rich in vitamins and fatty acids and is excellent as a natural moisturizer and emollient for dry or damaged hair.

4. Beeswax: Beeswax can be used to define hair textures and provide light hold. It is especially good for short hair or for shaping beard and mustache styling.

5. Jojoba oil: Jojoba oil is a light oil that resembles the natural sebum of the hair. It can be used as a hair oil, heat protectant or to reduce frizz.

6. Flaxseed gel: Flaxseed gel is a natural gel derived from flaxseed. It is excellent for defining curls, reducing frizz and as a light hold for all hair types.

7. Apple Cider Vinegar: Apple cider vinegar can be used as a natural hair spray to add shine and hold to hair. Simply mix apple cider vinegar and water in a ratio of 1:3 and apply to the hair with a spray bottle.

8. Argan oil: Argan oil is a rich, nourishing oil that gives shine and softness to the hair. It can be used as a hair oil or heat protection.

9. Salt spray: You can make a natural salt spray by mixing sea salt, water and a few drops of essential oil. Salt spray adds texture to the hair and a natural tousled beach look.

10. Hair gel from flaxseed: Boil flaxseed in water until it has a gel-like consistency. Strain it and let it cool. This gel can be used as a natural hair gel that provides hold and definition, especially for curly hair.

These natural styling products are a great alternative to chemical and synthetic products because they care for your hair while being kind to the environment.

However, if you use chemical hair styling products instead of natural products, I would recommend washing your hair before going to bed in any case. This will prevent the chemicals in the hair from causing long-term damage.

Now I share with you my secret recipe for hair styling:

I mix 100% natural organic lavender oil in an aloe vera spray and add the contents of 1-2 OPC capsules. Thus, I made fly massacre in one fell swoop. All of these remedies have very positive effects on the hair. The spray keeps my hair in style and smells very good. At first I used the spray without lavender oil, but I didn't like the smell. Then I got the idea to add lavender oil, because of its scent and benefits for the hair. Later, I added the contents of OPC capsules to make my own miracle product. If you want to try it too, make sure you don't have allergies to them.

For this I personally recommend these two products:

https://hawloo.eu/links/aloevera

https://hawloo.eu/links/lavendel

Scalp Care Through Massage

While I know that for many people (myself included) a head massage is considered a luxury, I still don't want to pass it up.

Regular scalp massage can have a variety of benefits for the scalp and hair. Massage can release energies in the scalp, helping to improve circulation and provide essential nutrients to the hair follicles. In addition, a scalp massage can also help to de-acidify the scalp, promote purification and detoxification, and improve the metabolism of the hair root.

It is recommended that massage be performed gently to avoid injury or damage to the scalp. Recommended massage techniques include stroking, light scratching, tapping and kneading. These techniques can help relieve tension in the scalp and create a pleasant feeling of relaxation. It is important to perform massage regularly to achieve the best results.

Detoxification And Relaxation Through Dry Brushing

Last but not least, for the sake of completeness, I would like to mention the brush massage.

The skin is the largest organ of the body and plays an important role in the elimination of acids and toxins. Regular supportive brushing massage helps the skin to promote self-regulation and increase the elimination of harmful substances. However, chemical skin care products can interfere with the skin's ability to excrete. Therefore, it is important to help the body deacidify and detoxify through regular dry brushing. Dry brushing opens the pores of the skin, improves circulation and makes the skin soft and supple. It also activates the lymphatic system, supporting faster transport and elimination of harmful substances. Dry brushing also has positive effects on the cardiovascular and nervous systems. To reap the health benefits of dry massage, skin should be carefully brushed before showering or bathing, avoiding injured skin areas and the face. The optimal brushing massage can be achieved with the monastery brush, whose special copper alloy bristles, when rubbed, generate a tiny current that relaxes the brushed areas and revitalizes the body.

This is the link to my recommended dry brush:

https://hawloo.eu/links/drybrushing

6) OTHER POSSIBLE NATURAL HEALING METHODS

Homeopathy as part of a holistic treatment

As I mentioned in my medical history, I have tried homeopathic therapies. Although I have not noticed any direct effects on my recovery, I would still like to share some important information. Homeopathic remedies are chosen depending on the cause of the hair loss. For example, China officinalis is recommended for hair loss following the birth of a child, while Natrium muriaticum is used for hair loss due to severe emotional stress such as breakups or the death of loved ones. In phytotherapy, evening primrose oil is recommended due to its high content of unsaturated fatty acids. In acupuncture, needles are placed specifically in the base of the hair to release energies and promote hair growth.

If it came down to considering homeopathic therapy, I would first do a thorough research before starting.

Tips against hair loss due to stress

Stress can lead to hair loss, especially diffuse hair loss. Stress hormones negatively affect the natural hair growth cycle and can lead to more hair falling out. To prevent hair loss, you should reduce or avoid stress.

I know it's easy to say. But in fact, it's not always easy to relieve stress, especially if you have a very busy work or study life. In your free time, you should therefore try to relax. There are various ways to do this, such as meditative exercises.

Exercise is also a good way to reduce stress. A combination of endurance and strength training three times a week at moderate intensity can help reduce stress. Regular exercise can prolong the hair growth cycle and improve hair health.

The influence of sleep rhythm on hair

Your hair can benefit greatly from a regular sleep schedule. Sleep is important because it gives your body a chance to recover and regenerate. If you sleep enough and have a stable sleep rhythm, it helps your body to function optimally, and this also has positive effects on your hair.

It is best to go to bed at the same time every night, if possible, taking into account the natural day-night rhythm. This means that it is ideal to go to bed a few hours after dark and adjust to the body's internal clock. If you manage to go to bed between 9pm and 11pm at night, you deserve a big congratulations from me.

The reason for this lies in the so-called circadian rhythm of the body, which controls our sleep-wake cycle. When you sleep in harmony with this internal clock, your body can work and recover more efficiently. This has very good effects on your hair health.

The early night hours are particularly important for regeneration, as increased growth hormones are released during this time. These hormones are essential for hair growth and cell renewal. The hair follicles are thus better supplied with nutrients and can renew themselves. Adequate and regular sleep supports your entire hormonal system.

So by paying attention to your body clock and going to sleep at the same time every night, you will help your body to regenerate optimally and thus also promote the growth and health of your hair.

Irregular sleep can cause hormonal imbalances that can lead to hair loss and poor hair quality. In addition, disturbed sleep patterns can also weaken the immune system, making the body more susceptible to infections and inflammation, which can also affect hair growth. For example, I remember that during the time when my disease started, I didn't sleep much at night and my sleep rhythm was disturbed. I wonder if that could possibly be the probable cause of my disease.

So make sure you get enough sleep every night and try to go to bed and get up at set times. This will help you maintain your sleep rhythm and give your body the best possible opportunity to take care of your hair health. Overall, a good sleep schedule can help your hair look stronger, healthier and shinier.

"THIS IS A MIRACLE" SAID MY DOCTOR
REVERSING HAIR LOSS AND ALOPECIA

AFTERWORD

In this book I have shared with you all my know-how and experience around hair health. I have tried not to leave out anything that I consider important, even if I have not implemented everything myself one-to-one. Honestly, I wanted to create a healthy hair growth manual for myself as well, because even I can forget some things sometimes. In addition, I want to use this book to express my gratitude to God. I hope that I have praised Him in some way in this book. Because ultimately, whether we are healed or not is up to God alone, regardless of the therapies we tackle. Nevertheless, the therapies we undertake are a kind of supplication to God, so we should not neglect them under any circumstances.

Yes, indeed, diseases and healings come equally from Him. You may ask: But why? That would be a separate book topic. But believe me, God is above all wickedness and shortcomings. He wants only the best for His creatures, as in my case. If He had not given me my illness at that time, I probably would not have had all these experiences and would not have been able to develop like this. It was a very difficult time, but I overcame it and created something good out of it, again with His help. Even this book is the result of my illness and healing. Who knows what good things this book will bring forth.

I believe that it is our responsibility to keep our entire body healthy. Since we humans are almost all born fit and healthy (there are exceptions, the cause of which is another topic), we have the responsibility to maintain our health as much as possible. In this regard, it is not only our hair that matters. Hair is only a certain part of this whole system. However, since everything is interconnected in this system, I would not neglect hair at all. Healthy hair is an indicator of a healthy body and vice versa. With this in mind, hopefully the application of the natural hair growth formula in this book will produce miraculous results. It should not be just a temporary cure, but part of our lifestyle.

Remain patient and persistent in your efforts. It will definitely be worth it. You can see good results after a few months, but bigger results can take 1 to 1.5 years.

Invitation to our Facebook Group

Since you have read this far, I want to thank you from the bottom of my heart for your interest. As a special surprise, I now invite you to become part of our multilingual Facebook group after reading the book. Here we offer a space for exchange in English, German and Turkish to continue the dialogue about the content, insights and experiences that the book evokes.

In our group, we are particularly concerned with creating an atmosphere of openness, respect, and mutual support. Your personal insights, lessons, and interpretations are invaluable in helping to inspire and enrich each other.

Please note that the group is specifically for discussions about the book and related topics. So I ask you to respect the group guidelines, respect other opinions, and contribute to a positive community.

I invite you now to join our group and exchange ideas with other readers. Together we can build an inspiring and supportive community that will follow us beyond the pages of the book.

Thank you again for your trust and participation. I look forward to welcoming you to our Facebook group and continuing the exchange with you.

,

https://www.facebook.com/groups/938061160784325/

Last but not least, dear reader:

After my healing, I now have another big challenge. I am seeking the cure for Stargardt's disease, not for myself, but for a person very close to me. Currently, modern medicine says that there is no cure for this. But I believe that the cure exists somewhere and we just need to find it. Should you come across a cure for this disease, I would be happy if you let me know about it.

I wish you all the best from the bottom of my heart.

Praise and thanks are due to the All-Glorious!

LIST OF SOURCES

[Anonymous]. Arteriosclerosis, Thrombosis, and Vascular Biology. Last accessed March 29, 2023.
https://www.ahajournals.org/doi/10.1161/ATVBAHA.112.248039

[Anonymous]. German Society for Orthomolecular Medicine. Last accessed March 29, 2023.
https://www.dgom.de/wissenswertes/kompendium/lebensnotwendige-molekuele/ascorbin

[Anonymous]. German Society for Orthomolecular Medicine. Last accessed March 29, 2023.
https://www.dgom.de/wissenswertes/kompendium/lebensnotwendige-molekuele/ascorbin

[Anonymous]. Focus Online. Last accessed [date omitted].
https://www.focus.de/gesundheit/ratgeber/haarausfall/news/silizium-verdickt-das-haar-haarqualitaet_id_1760280.html

[Anonymous]. Global Journal of Health Science. Last accessed March 29, 2023.
https://www.ccsenet.org/journal/index.php/gjhs/article/view/40015

[Anonymous]. The American Journal of Clinical Nutrition. Last accessed March 29, 2023.
https://academic.oup.com/ajcn/article/89/5/1686S/4596962?login=false

[Anonymous]. The American Journal of Clinical Nutrition. Last accessed March 29, 2023.
https://academic.oup.com/ajcn/article/89/5/1686S/4596962?login=false

[Anonymous]. The American Journal of Clinical Nutrition. Last accessed March 29, 2023. https://academic.oup.com/ajcn/article/75/5/887/4689403?login=false

[Online source]. 1998. https://pubmed.ncbi.nlm.nih.gov/9833041/.

[Online source]. 2006. https://journals.lww.com/jasn/pages/articleviewer.aspxyear=2006&issue=11000&article=00036&type=Fulltext.

[Online source]. 2007. https://pubmed.ncbi.nlm.nih.gov/17658124/.

[Online source]. 2011. https://pubmed.ncbi.nlm.nih.gov/21481501/.

[Online source]. n.d. http://www.haarausfall-therapie.net/natuerliche-haarausfallbehandlung.html.

[Online source]. n.d. http://www.opc-vitamin-p.com/.

[Online source]. n.d. https://www.yumpu.com/de/document/read/7118067/haarausfall-studie-joico-onlineshop-vicopura.

[Online source]. n.d. https://www.zentrum-der-gesundheit.de/bibliothek/medikamente/nebenwirkungen-medikamente/studien-pharmaindustrie.

[Online source]. n.d. https://www.zentrum-der-gesundheit.de/bibliothek/sonstige-informationen/medizin-und-forschung/wissenschaftliche-studien-medizin-ia.

[Online source]. n.d. https://www.zentrum-der-gesundheit.de/bibliothek/sonstige-informationen/medizin-und-forschung/wissenschaftliche-studien-faelschung-ia.

LIST OF SOURCES

[Online source]. n.d. https://www.zentrum-der-gesundheit.de/krankheiten/haare/haarausfall-uebersicht/glatzenbildung.

Buhârî. Tıbb 1, Ebu Dâvud, Tıbb 1, (3855); Tirmizî, Tıbb 2, (2039); İbnu Mâce, Tıbb 1, (3436).

Clemetson, C. A. B. "Histamine and ascorbic acid in human blood." Journal of Nutrition 110 (1980): 662-668.

Gillies, R., et al. "Bicarbonate Increases Tumor pH and Inhibits Spontaneous Metastases." Cancer Research, March 2009. https://aacrjournals.org/cancerres/article/69/6/2260/552860/Bicarbonate-Increases-Tumor-pH-and-Inhibits.

Goller, Werner. What is conventional medicine hiding? 2009.

Jentschura, Dr.h.c.. Peter, and Josef Lohkämper. Health through purification. May 2010.

Ludwig Institute for Cancer Research. "How might baking soda boost cancer therapy? Researchers describe how acidity turns oxygen-starved cancer cells dormant and drug resistant -- and a potentially easy way reverse the effect." ScienceDaily, June 1, 2018.

Medical College of Georgia at Augusta University. "Drinking baking soda could be an inexpensive, safe way to combat autoimmune disease: A daily dose of baking soda may help reduce the destructive inflammation of autoimmune diseases like rheumatoid arthritis, scientists say." ScienceDaily, April 25, 2018.

Musall, Hiram Ocasio, Debra Irsik, Jessica A. Filosa, Jennifer C. Sullivan, Brendan Marshall, Ryan A. Harris, and Paul M. O'Connor. "Oral NaHCO3 Activates a Splenic Anti-Inflammatory Pathway: Evidence That Cholinergic Signals Are Transmitted via Mesothelial

Cells." The Journal of Immunology, 2018; 1701605.
https://journals.aai.org/jimmunol/article/200/10/3568/106666/Or
al-NaHCO3-Activates-a-Splenic-Anti-Inflammatory.

Price, K. D., Price, C. S. C., & Reynolds, R. D. "Hyperglycemia-
induced latent scurvy and atherosclerosis: the scorbutic-metaplasia
hypothesis." Medical Hypotheses 46, no. 2 (1996): 119-129.

Simons, Anne, and Alexander Rucker. "Living healthier longer with
OPC." 2005, 68.

Simons, Anne, and Alexander Rucker. "Living healthier longer with
OPC." 2005, 10.

Simons, Anne, and Alexander Rucker. Healthy Living Longer with
OPC. 2005.

Walton, Zandra E., Chi V. Dang, et al. "Acid Suspends the Circadian
Clock in Hypoxia through Inhibition of TOR." Cell, May 31, 2018.

Health Center. "Colon Cleanse." https://www.zentrum-der-
gesundheit.de/b.

Health Center. "Liver Cleanse." https://www.zentrum-der-
gesundheit.de/bibliothek/koerper/leber-und-galle/leberreinigung.

Health Center. "Lymphatic Cleansing." https://www.zentrum-der-
gesundheit.de/bibliothek/naturheilkunde/gesundheitskuren/lymph
e-reinigen.

Health Center. "Master Cleanse." https://www.zentrum-der-
gesundheit.de/bibliothek/naturheilkunde/gesundheitskuren/maste
r-cleanse.

Health Center. "Kidney Cleanse." https://www.zentrum-der-
gesundheit.de/bibliothek/naturheilkunde/gesundheitskuren/niere
nreinigung.

Health Center. "Pseudo Liver Cleanse." https://www.zentrum-der-gesundheit.de/bibliothek/ratgeber/detox-uebersicht/pseudo-leberreinigung.

Health Center. "Lemon Garlic Cure." https://www.zentrum-der-gesundheit.de/bibliothek/ratgeber/detox-uebersicht/zitronen-knoblauch-kur.

Ziemann, B., and Enzmann, F. Vitamin C ascorbic acid: a vital protective factor. MSE, 1998.

[Anonymous]. Linus Pauling Institute. Last accessed March 29, 2023. https://lpi.oregonstate.edu/mic/vitamins/biotin

[Anonymous]. Linus Pauling Institute. Last accessed March 29, 2023. https://lpi.oregonstate.edu/mic/vitamins/vitamin-C

[Anonymous]. British Journal of Cancer. Last accessed March 29, 2023. https://www.nature.com/articles/bjc2014294

Goller, Werner. "What is conventional medicine hiding?" 2009, 10.

[Anonymous]. Clinical Cancer Research. Last accessed March 29, 2023. https://aacrjournals.org/clincancerres/article/12/20/6194/191679/Grape-Seed-Extract-Inhibits-In-vitro-and-In-vivo

[Anonymous]. German Nutrition Society. Last accessed March 29, 2023. https://www.dge.de/wissenschaft/referenzwerte/biotin/?L=0

[Anonymous]. National Institutes of Health. Last accessed March 29, 2023. https://ods.od.nih.gov/factsheets/VitaminC-Consumer/

[Anonymous]. Cancer Prevention Research. Last accessed March 29, 2023.

https://aacrjournals.org/cancerpreventionresearch/article/12/8/55
7/47242/A-Pilot-Study-of-a-Grape-Seed-Procyanidin-Extract

[Anonymous]. Health with Nature. Last accessed March 29, 2023.
https://healthwithnature.de/vitamine.shtml

[Anonymous]. JAMA Network Open. Last accessed March 29, 2023.
https://jamanetwork.com/journals/jamanetworkopen/fullarticle/2
770157

[Anonymous]. Hamburg Medical Laboratory. Last accessed March
29, 2023.
https://www.mlhb.de/fileadmin/user_upload/Startseite/Service/La
borinformationen/Vitamin_C_0216.pdf

[Anonymous]. NIHR Journals Library. Last accessed March 29,
2023.
https://www.journalslibrary.nihr.ac.uk/hta/hta23020#/abstract

[Anonymous]. Oxford Academic. Last accessed March 29, 2023.
https://academic.oup.com/carcin/article/20/9/1737/261642?login
=false

[Anonymous]. PLOS ONE. Last accessed March 29, 2023.
https://journals.plos.org/plosone

[Anonymous]. PubMed Central. Last accessed March 29, 2023.
https://www.ncbi.nlm.nih.gov/pmc/articles/PMC6835439/

[Anonymous]. PubMed Central. Last accessed March 29, 2023.
https://www.ncbi.nlm.nih.gov/pmc/articles/PMC6071228/

[Anonymous]. PubMed Central. Last accessed March 29, 2023.
https://www.ncbi.nlm.nih.gov/pmc/articles/PMC3025097/

[Anonymous]. PubMed Central. Last accessed March 29, 2023.
https://www.ncbi.nlm.nih.gov/pmc/articles/PMC3622127/

[Anonymous]. PubMed. Last accessed March 29, 2023.
https://pubmed.ncbi.nlm.nih.gov/25057538/

[Anonymous]. PubMed. Last accessed March 29, 2023.
https://pubmed.ncbi.nlm.nih.gov/28879195/

[Anonymous]. PubMed. Last accessed March 29, 2023.
https://pubmed.ncbi.nlm.nih.gov/21979243/

[Anonymous]. PubMed. Last accessed March 29, 2023.
https://pubmed.ncbi.nlm.nih.gov/11896744/

[Anonymous]. PubMed. Last accessed March 29, 2023.
https://pubmed.ncbi.nlm.nih.gov/29099763/

[Anonymous]. PubMed. Last accessed March 29, 2023.
https://pubmed.ncbi.nlm.nih.gov/28338764/

[Anonymous]. PubMed. Last accessed March 29, 2023.
https://pubmed.ncbi.nlm.nih.gov/26227083/

[Anonymous]. PubMed. Last accessed March 29, 2023.
https://pubmed.ncbi.nlm.nih.gov/8692035/

[Anonymous]. PubMed. Last accessed March 29, 2023.
https://pubmed.ncbi.nlm.nih.gov/19508394/

[Anonymous]. PubMed. Last accessed March 29, 2023.
https://pubmed.ncbi.nlm.nih.gov/12134712/

[Anonymous]. PubMed. Last accessed March 29, 2023.
https://pubmed.ncbi.nlm.nih.gov/3917362/

[Anonymous]. PubMed. Last accessed March 29, 2023.
https://pubmed.ncbi.nlm.nih.gov/12771534/

[Anonymous]. PubMed. Last accessed March 29, 2023.

https://pubmed.ncbi.nlm.nih.gov/9833041/

[Anonymous]. PubMed. Last accessed March 29, 2023.
https://pubmed.ncbi.nlm.nih.gov/9090754/

[Anonymous]. ScienceDirect. Last accessed March 29, 2023.
https://www.sciencedirect.com/science/article/abs/pii/S0300483X00002109?via%3Dihub

[Anonymous]. ScienceDirect. Last accessed March 29, 2023.
https://www.sciencedirect.com/science/article/abs/pii/S030438350700403X?via%3Dihub

[Anonymous]. Springer Link. Last accessed March 29, 2023.
https://link.springer.com/article/10.1007/s002160051243

[Anonymous]. SpringerLink. Last accessed March 29, 2023.
https://link.springer.com/article/10.1007/s12603-014-0020-8

[Anonymous]. SpringerLink. Last accessed March 29, 2023.
https://link.springer.com/article/10.1007/s13197-019-04113-w

[Anonymous]. Wiley Online Library. Last accessed March 29, 2023.
https://onlinelibrary.wiley.com/doi/10.1111/jocd.13711

[Anonymous]. Center for Health. Last accessed March 29, 2023.
https://www.zentrum-der-gesundheit.de/pdf/tabelle_lebensmittel_mit_vitamin_c.pdf

[Anonymous]. PubMed Central. Last accessed March 30, 2023.
https://www.ncbi.nlm.nih.gov/pmc/articles/PMC2906676/

Disclaimer

Neither this book nor the content provided in this book and on the website (https://hawloo.eu) should in any way be construed as medical advice or medical treatment.

All products linked and recommended in my book and website are food supplements / dietary supplement (CH) (except the drugs prescribed by the author's doctor). Food supplement / dietary supplement (CH) should not be used as a substitute for a balanced and varied diet and healthy lifestyle. Do not exceed the specified recommended daily intake. Storage of dietary supplements / food supplements (CH) should always be out of reach of small children. When taking dietary supplements / nutritional supplement (CH), responsible use is crucial to avoid side effects. Furthermore, known intolerances to certain ingredients must also be considered before taking. However, should side effects or health damage occur due to individual intolerances, the author, Selim Dursun, assumes no liability.

The information in this book and on our website (https://hawloo.eu) is intended to supplement, not replace, the advice of your physician or healthcare provider. You should therefore never use the information provided here as your sole source for making health-related decisions. If you have any complaints, you should always seek medical advice. The texts do not claim to be complete, nor can the timeliness, accuracy and balance of the information presented be guaranteed.

The texts in no way replace the professional advice of a doctor or pharmacist and may not be used as a basis for independent diagnosis and the beginning, modification or termination of treatment of diseases or as a prevention of such.

The author, Selim Dursun, assumes no liability for any inconvenience or damage resulting from the use of the information presented here.

Copyright © 2023

Selim Dursun
Fichtestr. 65
63303 Dreieich
Web: https://hawloo.eu
E-Mail: info@hawloo.eu

THIS WORK IS PROTECTED BY COPYRIGHT.
All rights, including those of translation, reprinting and reproduction of the work or parts thereof, are reserved. No part of this work may be reproduced in any form (photocopy, microfilm or any other process) or processed, duplicated or distributed using electronic systems without the written permission of the publisher, not even for the purpose of teaching.

The reproduction of common names, trade names, product designations, etc. in this work, even without special identification, does not justify the assumption that such names would be considered free within the meaning of trademark and brand protection legislation and may therefore be used by anyone. Despite careful proofreading, errors may creep in. The author and publisher are therefore grateful for any comments in this regard. Any liability is excluded, all rights reserved.

© 2023 Selim Dursun
Edition 1
Author: Selim Dursun

IMAGE RIGHTS & LICENSES:
All images used in this book are my property and are subject to my copyright. Any unauthorized use, reproduction or distribution of these images is prohibited. Any imitation or unlawful use will be prosecuted.

www.ingramcontent.com/pod-product-compliance
Lightning Source LLC
LaVergne TN
LVHW020318200726
843507LV00012B/2157

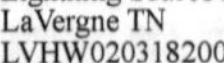